THE PROMOTION THAT CHANGED EVERYTHING

A Business Fable for Defeating Impostor Syndrome with Positive Psychology

by

RENEE BRUNS, DBA

For everyone who is tired of faking it.

Table of Contents

Note from the Author

It took me 20 years of working in corporate America, plus another four years of doctoral research, to realize how severely I have struggled with impostor syndrome my entire life. But through my four years of doctoral research, I learned that I don't have to live like an impostor forever.

I spent four years studying the impacts of impostor syndrome on one's job, career, life, and health. The effects are disheartening and real.

I also spent four years studying how the practice of positive psychology can reverse those feelings. It *is* possible to defeat impostor syndrome.

As I told people, family, friends, and strangers, about my doctoral research, I received a resounding response: "Oh my gosh, I have impostor syndrome. Tell me more about positive psychology. Could it help me?"

Both topics are deeply studied, and it would be impossible to put the research that both subjects have received into one book. But I also know that there are more people than I could ever know who need to learn about both topics.

This book, a short fable designed for any reader, is intentionally short. The topics are high-level and basic, but they are a foundation to help anyone who wants to feel more empowered and capable get started on a path towards a more authentic and less exhausting future.

I will see you, the *real* you, on the other side of impostor syndrome.

Renee

What is Impostor Syndrome and Do I Have It?

Miranda pulled up to her office building, a five-story high-rise building on the outskirts of Omaha, Nebraska. It was a cold but sunny Monday, and Miranda was looking forward to the week ahead. She loved her job and her team, and most days, she just wanted to be at work.

It was around 10 am, after two cups of coffee and a few hours of cleaning up her email inbox, when Miranda's boss, Tom, entered her office.

"Good morning, Miranda. How are you today?"

"Hi Tom. I'm doing well. It's been a productive morning. How are you?"

Tom shut the door behind him, and Miranda panicked. What did she do? Was this it? Was she going to be fired? She'd worried about being terminated her entire career.

"I just found out that Nina will be moving to another department." Tom went on to say. "Which means that her position is now open. I'd like you to take her role."

Miranda's heart skipped a beat. Nina was a *director*. There was no way Miranda was ready for a *director* role. Did Tom really mean to offer her this job?

Her first instinct was to ask him: "Do you really think I'm ready for that big of a role?" But she stopped herself. She didn't want Tom to know she was barely qualified for her current role, where she managed a team of 15 employees. The director's role was much bigger; she would be leading 50 people. What if he found out she was "faking it" in her current role the entire time? What if he found out that she had no idea what she was doing? Then he might demote her, or, even worse, fire her for misleading him about her skills.

But she also wanted the promotion. It was a dream ever since she was a little girl. She had worked hard, both in her career and in her outside educational pursuits, to become a great leader.

She rationalized with herself. She just *knew* she wasn't qualified. She could feel it in her bones. So, if she accepted this job, she would have to work extra hard to prove herself and to make up for all of her shortcomings.

Tom sat in the chair across from her desk, his arms slightly crossed in front of him and waited for a few seconds while Miranda quickly processed her thoughts. She had been working with him for over five years and knew his personality and management style quite well. If Tom was offering her the job, he wasn't going to let her say no. He'd made up his mind that she

2

was the person to do the job, and there were no other candidates. The job was hers; all she had to do was say yes.

"Oh my gosh," she calmly said on the outside, her heart racing and the voice inside her head trembling with fear. "Thank you for thinking of me. I won't disappoint you."

They talked briefly about what her transition to the new role in just a week would look like. She rigorously took notes, excitement and fear flooding her emotions. When he finally turned to leave her office, she thanked him one more time and gripped the edge of her desk. Was she really going to be a director? What had she gotten herself into?

A few days later, when she received the very formal offer letter in her email, a formality that she would need to electronically sign and return to HR, she saw her new salary. She and Tom had spoken about her new compensation when she accepted the job, but seeing it on paper made it real. It was validation that this was a *big* role. Miranda was overwhelmed with fear and regret. This was too large a role for her, and the offer letter confirmed that. How was she going to fake her way through this?

Miranda immediately made an appointment with her therapist. She had been working with a therapist for many years, and it always helped her when life got tough. She had struggled with high anxiety her entire life and had bouts of depression that brought her to dark places every few years, a remnant from a difficult childhood she was trying to heal from. She was elated to share the news of her promotion with her therapist. She was quietly a little excited, but mostly petrified that she was going to let her boss down. And she couldn't let Tom know about this. All of this, everything, and every time she pretended to be or do something else, had gotten her to this point. Now, overselling herself was just yet another thing that she overexaggerated to get herself into this position.

Miranda spent a few sessions working with her therapist to understand why she was so afraid of this new role. They used many of the same psychotherapy practices they had in the past; the sessions were fruitful, and Miranda felt better, but she still couldn't understand how she was going to enjoy the new job and do it well when she had to go to work every day feeling like a fake. Her therapist gave her the reassurance she needed that she could do the job and promised to continue working with her. She also suggested that Miranda hire a business leadership coach to help her with this career transition.

A week later, Miranda met Omar, a leadership coach with over twenty years of experience. She was sitting in her home office, a blanket on her lap, as she logged in to the video-chatting platform. It was her last meeting of the day. They introduced themselves, and Omar asked Miranda to tell him about her career to date and why she was seeking his services.

She went into great detail about her education, various positions, and the new director role that she had just accepted. She explained to Omar that she needed his help because she wanted to be the best leader she could be, but she wasn't sure how to do that and wasn't even sure if she could.

Omar asked Miranda to elaborate on why she didn't think she could do the job if she was offered it…*and* accepted it.

"Well, I don't really know, Omar. I've just advanced so quickly in my career. I just got a promotion last year, and the year before that, too. I feel like I'm still learning my current role. There's no way I'm ready to be a *director*."

Omar nodded, and Miranda continued.

"I think I just got lucky, and that Tom has to fill this role fast, and there's no one else who will take it. Maybe I should have told him no…" Miranda said, disappointment with herself hung in her voice.

"Honestly, I'm afraid that the new responsibilities will be too much. I'm finally figuring out my current job, but if Tom thinks I can do the new job to the same caliber, he's just wrong. I have no idea what I'm doing. I would have *never* considered this job if Tom hadn't come to me directly and basically told me I was going to do it."

Miranda talked and talked and talked about her fears of this new role for over 45 minutes. She felt better just explaining how she felt to Omar. He was patient, understanding, and a great listener. At the end of their first session, where Miranda did most of the talking, he asked, "Miranda, have you ever heard of impostor syndrome?"

"Impostor syndrome? No… I've never heard that term before." Miranda said with an inquisitive tone.

"Well, what I think you're struggling with, it actually has a lot of names. And it goes back to 1978, when two researchers, Pauline Rose Clance and Suzanne Imes, coined the term.[i] They originally called it impostor phenomenon when they first researched individuals with these characteristics, some of the same things you are describing to me. Some people call it fraud syndrome, or impostor experience, or perceived fraudulence. I like impostor syndrome, but it doesn't really matter what you call it. The *concept* and the *characteristics* are the same."

"Wow," Miranda blurted out. "So, this…impostor syndrome, or whatever name you call it, has been around for quite some time. That's interesting. But what *is* impostor syndrome? How do you know I have it?"

"Well, in a nutshell, impostor syndrome, that's the phrase I prefer, is an unhealthy response to success."

"An unhealthy response to success? Omar, you think that I'm having an unhealthy response to success? I don't understand. I just accepted a big promotion." Miranda blurted out, upset that Omar accused her of being unhealthy.

"Miranda…" Omar tried to calm her down. "Hear me out, and please don't get upset. None of this is your fault…and you're not alone."

Miranda took a deep breath and nodded, indicating that Omar should continue.

"Individuals who struggle with impostor syndrome often believe that they got into the position they are in by faking it. They don't believe that they are as smart as they are or as capable as they are, and they are convinced that someone is going to figure out that they are a fraud, fake, or, hence the term, impostor. They are just *waiting* for someone to figure out that they didn't *actually* earn their success. People who struggle with impostor syndrome think they 'just got lucky.' One of the first things you told me about your new promotion is that you didn't think you deserved it, and that you were afraid your boss, Tom, was going to realize soon that you aren't as capable as you are. Isn't that right?"

"Yes," Miranda said, feeling like Omar was onto something.

"Another characteristic of impostor syndrome is the inability to celebrate one's own success. In the past 45 minutes, during the entire conversation about your career, not once did you mention anything about being proud of yourself and doing something to celebrate your promotion. You haven't been able to see any joy in what you've accomplished. Aren't you proud of yourself?" Omar inquired.

"Well, yes… But I'm afraid I'm going to let down my entire team, that we'll all fail together, and so I don't want to celebrate any victories yet. Honestly, Omar, I just don't think Tom knows who I am," Miranda explained.

"Another classic characteristic of impostor syndrome: a fear of being judged by others if you should fail, or in other words, a fear of being successful. Ironically, you've been able to successfully grow your former team. Why wouldn't you be able to do that again, in this new role?" Omar questioned.

"I don't know. I think I just got lucky with my previous team."

Omar firmly stated, "Exactly, you *think* you got lucky and won't be able to repeat the success. This is yet another characteristic of someone with impostor syndrome."

"Do you see how these are all unhealthy responses to success?" Omar leaned his head to the side, waiting for Miranda's response.

"Yes, I do. I suppose I haven't done a very good job at recognizing my own capability." Miranda confirmed, a hint of disappointment in her voice.

"Miranda," Omar said calmly. "I don't want you to feel bad about this. That's why you're here - to defeat these feelings. You don't have to live like this, always afraid of being caught, never being able to enjoy your success. You deserve to live authentically and to be yourself."

Miranda nodded, feeling like she had found someone who understood her, at least. Together, they were going to defeat this.

"I want to explain the different types of impostors that there are. These were all identified by Dr. Valerie Young.[ii] She's an excellent researcher if you want to learn more about impostor syndrome. She's identified five types of impostors.

"The first is a **perfectionist**. You can probably guess what this means: someone who will not submit a project or task until it's perfect. Perfectionists often don't want to, or don't have time to, take on new projects or tasks because they are always trying to perfect the current project. It becomes debilitating, and they set themselves up for failure.

"The second is the **superhero**. A superhero is different from a perfectionist in that they think they can handle everything. If someone asks them to help on a project, they say yes, even if they know they don't have time. A superhero will 'figure out' how to get it done, and when they inevitably fail, because they took on too much, they feel shame.

"The third is a **natural genius**. A natural genius is someone who seems to naturally grasp new things and is generally successful at all things they do. However, when they do inevitably struggle with something—we all do, we're human—they attribute it to failure on their part.

"The **expert** is the fourth type. This type of impostor believes they know everything. Like the natural genius, when they eventually run into an area where they are not an expert, they blame themselves for their shortcomings and lack of knowledge.

"Finally, the **soloist** is someone who believes they are capable of doing all things on their own. They never ask for help and believe that needing help is a sign of failure. What do you think?"

Miranda was vigorously taking notes. "Well, Omar, I think I have some of all of these characteristics. That's not good, is it?"

"Don't beat yourself up, Miranda. We are all human, and we probably all have some of these characteristics. It's when they become overpowering that it becomes a problem. And that's why you're here, right?"

"Yes, that's right. What else can you tell me about impostor syndrome?"

Omar continued. "You'll probably be surprised to learn how much impostor syndrome impacts other areas of a person's career… and life. Its impacts are much more than just the feelings you have inside right now."

"What do you mean?"

"Individuals with impostor syndrome generally have lower job satisfaction *and* lower career satisfaction. Think about that if you are struggling with impostor syndrome, in general, you are less satisfied with your job *and* your overall career."

"Wow… I've had a great career, better than I ever expected to. I can't imagine going further than this. This is interesting!" Miranda exclaimed.

"There's more…" Omar stated. "Individuals who struggle with impostor syndrome have lower life satisfaction, too. They are generally more exhausted – mostly attributed to the large amounts of energy they exude trying to 'hide' themselves and cover up from being 'fake.' This leads to increased cases of burnout, *and* their overall health is lower than that of their peers."

"Oh my gosh." Omar could see the shock on Miranda's face.

"Now, Miranda, we've only talked about the impacts of impostor syndrome related to you or an individual. But you are now leading a large team. Fifty or so people, right?"

Miranda nodded.

"The thing about impostor syndrome is that many people don't know they are struggling with it. Like you, you didn't understand it until today. Most people would look at you from the outside and think that you have it totally together, you know exactly what you are doing. You appear to be so confident. Am I right?"

"Yes."

"Well, if that's true of you, do you think it's possible that there are people on your team feeling the exact same way as you are, trying to cover up their success, and afraid of being caught? Do you think there are people on your team who also have impostor syndrome?"

"Well, yes, I suppose that's possible."

"The research on impostor syndrome suggests that impostor syndrome can impact anyone.[iii, iv] It doesn't discriminate against a specific demographic or position in a company. That means that *anyone*, regardless of gender, race, ethnicity, religion, or even their position in the company, can have impostor syndrome."

"Really? But my boss, Tom, for example, is so confident all the time. He couldn't possibly have impostor syndrome."

"Well, he might not. That's true. But it is not uncommon for leaders at the top of an organization to also struggle with it; they're just really good at covering it up. And you know the worst part about that? Because they often have less of a peer group (there are fewer leaders at the top), they feel even more alone and can't talk about their feelings with anyone," Omar explained.

Omar went on. "I want you to think about the impacts of impostor syndrome now, specific to your team, and not just yourself. If there are other people on your team who struggle with it, how might that impact your team on a larger scale?"

"Well, I mean, if someone isn't happy with their job, they're probably not going to be performing as well as they could. My team's results could suffer, and they might even start looking for a new job."

"Exactly," Omar commented. "And someone struggling with impostor syndrome often isn't as effective at completing tasks. They often procrastinate, thinking they aren't qualified to complete the task in the first place, or they overprepare, trying to be sure the task is completed to the expectations they set for themselves, which are often unrealistic and unachievable."

"Yes, that's a good point. I think I do that myself. I'm the worst at procrastinating." Miranda chimed in before adding more.

"Also, if an employee suffers from impostor syndrome, they probably aren't going to be a good mentor to others on their team, or to new employees. They could even teach the habits of the syndrome to others. For example, if a mentor struggles with impostor syndrome and they are mentoring a new employee, they might express that it's impossible to have actually earned or achieved the career they have. Those negative thought processes could be ingrained in the new employee's mind, and thus, a culture of impostor syndrome is created. Or if the mentor is constantly talking about finding a new job because they have low job satisfaction, their mentee will start to believe they need to feel the same. This could create a really difficult situation when it comes to succession planning. Is that true? Do I understand the impact of impostor syndrome on an organization correctly?"

"Yes, you do. Very good. It is very common for organizations as a whole to struggle with impostor syndrome. Often, organizational cultures create these dynamics without even knowing it. Part of that perpetuating problem stems from a person not feeling comfortable about sharing their feelings. If they aren't comfortable sharing their feelings, they are unlikely to feel comfortable sharing new ideas. So, if one person in an organization struggles with impostor syndrome, it can ultimately have impacts on everyone around them."

Miranda nodded. "Yes, that's such a good point. And if it's true that employees with impostor syndrome are more exhausted because they are working 'extra hard' to hide it, that will definitely impact their productivity, and ultimately my team's results. Of course, I also want my team to be healthy, not exhausted, for a lot of reasons, less expense, less time off, and mostly, healthy employees are better employees and better people."

Omar nodded with satisfaction that Miranda was grasping the larger impacts, beyond just herself.

"I know it's not part of my job description, but I also care about the general well-being of my employees. I want them to be generally happy, healthy, and satisfied with their life, so if impostor syndrome is decreasing all of those things, I want to do something about that."

Omar smiled again.

"Wow," Miranda stated factually. She had a lot to process. "Thank you, Omar. This has been so informative. I'm really glad you are here to help me."

That night, as Miranda was watching spaghetti noodles boil on her stove, she reflected on what Omar had taught her about impostor syndrome. She didn't like that impostor syndrome even existed. *How unfair,* she thought to herself. She reflected back on her entire career and thought of all the times that she didn't speak up in meetings because she was afraid that her ideas weren't strong enough. She thought of all the times that she wanted to

13

apply for a job—a promotion—but convinced herself she wasn't qualified. She thought of all the times that she hadn't allowed herself to feel successful because she felt like she had just gotten lucky and it wouldn't happen again.

As Miranda warmed up her homemade marinara sauce, she wondered what her career would have looked like if she *didn't* have impostor syndrome. Miranda started to think of all the people she'd encountered throughout her career, and wondered how many of them also struggled with impostor syndrome (and maybe didn't even know it). What would her company, or the world, be like if everyone was able to defeat impostor syndrome?

What Caused It and How Can I Get Rid of It?

It was now clear to Miranda that she had impostor syndrome. She knew she struggled with it after her first session with Omar. Everything they talked about fit her feelings to a tee. But she didn't like it and wanted to do everything she could to defeat impostor syndrome.

And then there was also her team. If there were individuals who struggled with impostor syndrome working under her leadership, she wanted to help them defeat impostor syndrome, too. She knew it was going to take some individuality *and* teamwork.

But before she figured out how she was going to tackle this, she wanted to understand how and why she, and others, have impostor syndrome. In her next session with Omar, she asked right away. "Omar, I've been thinking about impostor syndrome. I've accepted that this is something I might have, but what caused it? Why do *I* have it? What did I do wrong to get this?"

Omar sat in his typical blue desk chair, with an array of plants in his background. It was clear he loved his plants, and Miranda quietly admired his dedication. They made her sessions all the more welcoming. Omar answered Miranda right away and went on to explain that there are a lot of reasons why people might struggle with impostor syndrome.

"For starters, we need to remember the biology of human beings. There are some theories that suggest that we, humans, underestimate our abilities as a survival mechanism. If we underestimate our abilities, it protects us and helps to maintain social order. However, over time, we've adapted and evolved, and those needs to protect ourselves have changed. This is just a theory, but it's an interesting point and something to remember. We *are* just human."

Miranda nodded. This was a good reminder: she and her team are only human.

"There is also some research suggesting that people with high anxiety, depression, and/or low self-esteem are more prone to impostor syndrome.[v] This doesn't mean that someone with high anxiety, depression, or low self-esteem always suffers from impostor syndrome, and it doesn't mean that someone with impostor syndrome has mental health struggles either. In fact, there's not even a clinical diagnosis for impostor syndrome, and it's not recognized as a psychiatric disorder the way anxiety or depression are. But there is often a correlation between impostor syndrome and the other disorders."

"That's really interesting, Omar. I've struggled with anxiety and depression, at various points, for my entire life." Miranda confirmed.

Omar smiled, confirming Miranda's sentiment. He went on, "An individual's upbringing can also influence impostor syndrome in adulthood[i].."

"How so?" Miranda asked.

"Well, for example, let's say you had a younger sister, but she never received as good grades as you, and you were always the star athlete. If your parents started expecting you to always have straight As and finish first in your running races, you would start to feel the immense pressure to meet their expectations. And because of that, you would constantly be afraid of letting them down or failing. As a child, you didn't do anything different than your younger sister, who was also an excellent student and athlete, but just not quite as strong an achiever as you. Because you had the same parents and home life, you started to believe that your success was just luck and that you would soon fail a test or miss a race. You were just *waiting* for your parents to figure out that you aren't actually as good a kid as they thought."

"That makes so much sense."

Omar continued. "The ironic part is that your younger sister could also develop impostor syndrome. Because she started receiving the message that she wasn't good enough, or as strong a student or athlete as you, anytime she did have a stellar grade or an athletic achievement, she too believed it was because of luck."

"Oh wow," Miranda said. "I don't have a younger sibling, so this doesn't apply to me, but that's really interesting."

"Isn't it?" Omar confirmed. "Another indicator of impostor syndrome is being in a super competitive environment. Individuals who work in highly competitive environments where they are constantly being compared to their peers are often more likely have impostor syndrome. That brings me to my next point: comparing ourselves to others."

Miranda smiled. She knew she did this way too often.

"How often do you use social media? And when you do, do you ever find yourself comparing your life to someone else's?"[vi]

Miranda just kept smiling. There was no need to respond; they both knew the answer. She knew she had to cut back on her social media use. Every time she found herself on a social media app, she couldn't help but wonder how other women were pulling off great careers, happy marriages, and raising a family. She was doing the same things as them, but it didn't feel like she was doing it so gracefully. She didn't post pictures of herself in the morning, her hair in a messy bun, and coffee spilt on her shirt. She just assumed other women were much more capable of handling their obligations (even though deep down she knew better). Omar was right. She needed to stop comparing herself, and one way to do that was to cut back on social media. There was no better time than now.

"I can tell that you don't think we need to talk at length about comparing ourselves to other people, but know that it applies outside of social media, too. It can happen in the workplace, in your friends' circles, and even in your family. We all do it; it's part of being human. But there seems to be a correlation between comparing ourselves to others and impostor syndrome."

Omar paused. "Is this helping to explain how or what causes impostor syndrome?"

"Yes, it really is. Are there other indicators?" Miranda felt like some of this applied to her, but not everything, and she wanted to make sure she had as much information as possible.

"Yes, there are. People who struggle with perfectionism often also struggle with impostor syndrome. In addition, individuals who don't like being praised for their success often struggle with impostor syndrome. Since they often believe their success was just luck, they feel that having attention on them could bring light to the fact that they are faking it, or that they are an impostor and have no idea what they are doing. They try to avoid any praise or recognition so that they are not caught faking it."

He continued on. "People with impostor syndrome are often high performers, because they overwork to hide their self-believed inadequacies, sometimes to the point of burnout. They become so preoccupied with what others will think of them and others' expectations that they are constantly balancing how high to set their own bar. They know they can set it quite high, but if they set a big goal and achieve it, then they will be expected to complete an even bigger goal next time. And because they never actually believed they were capable, they live in constant fear of failing. The solution for many? Work extra hard to prove themselves, despite the fact that they have already done that."

"Yep, that's me," Miranda confirmed, wondering if she'd ever be able to *not* overwork. Overworking is what she did to become so successful. "What else?"

"Well, the science indicates that anyone can be impacted by impostor syndrome [iii], [iv]. Remember, we talked about that in our last session?"

"Yes."

"And that is true. However, there is some conflicting research that suggests minority groups might be impacted more.[vii] It's difficult to confirm because in most organizations, there tends to be some degree of homogeneity. For example, a call center might have a predominantly younger generation that is white and female, depending on geographic location and population makeup. If an older white man began working there, he might experience some impostor syndrome because he doesn't mirror the demographic of the larger group. Does that make sense?"

"Yes, so basically anyone can be impacted, but if an individual doesn't fit into the larger population or team, they might experience impostor syndrome in that setting more than the others." Miranda restated her understanding.

"Yes, that's exactly right."

"Okay, but in this example, the man is older and probably more experienced. Why would he have impostor syndrome?"

"That's a great question. And it stems from not 'fitting in.' Because he is less like the majority – in this case, he would be the minority – impostor syndrome can sneak in."

"That's really interesting. I wouldn't have expected someone with more experience to feel impostor syndrome." Miranda said as she scribbled on her notepad.

"Right. And I also want to point out that different cultures from around the world can influence one's experience with impostor syndrome."

Miranda nodded in confirmation.

"Like different cultural experiences, customs, and traditions, it's important to understand that each person has a lifetime of events in their past. Life experiences and trauma can certainly impact impostor syndrome. That's a big topic, and too large for us to get into, but let's just leave it at this: trauma can impact the severity of impostor syndrome."

"Got it." Miranda couldn't agree more. She had her own trauma from her childhood that she didn't want or need to discuss with Omar, but she understood that those traumas could be impacting her impostor syndrome.

"Miranda," Omar said. "There are a lot of reasons people experience impostor syndrome. As we've discussed, some are very obvious, and then there are reasons a person might have impostor syndrome, but there's no explanation for why. The important part is that they receive tools to alleviate it. Don't you agree?"

"Yes. Yes, Omar, I agree completely. So how does one… get rid of it? Is that the right way to look at it? How do I get rid of impostor syndrome?"

"Not necessarily, but you're on the right track. Research shows that an individual can rarely 'get rid of' impostor syndrome completely.[viii] It never really goes away. But instead, with time and implementation of various techniques, it can diminish, and individuals can manage it to the point where it no longer impacts their day-to-day jobs, careers, or lives."

Miranda was a bit disappointed. She really wanted to rid herself of these feelings…forever. Omar was telling her that it wasn't possible, though. Learning about impostor syndrome alone gave Miranda great relief, and she knew she was not alone. For the first time, she had a sudden sense of hope – something she didn't have before – from Omar that she was going to defeat impostor syndrome. And that alone was comforting.

"Okay," Miranda said, knowing she was ready to jump in and do everything she could to manage her impostor syndrome and make it diminish.

"Often, I find that the first step in defeating impostor syndrome is simply acknowledging it. You've done that already."

Miranda smiled.

"I've found that acknowledging its presence, talking about it, and accepting that it's part of who you are are the keys to successfully tackling impostor syndrome. And you've done all of those things."

"I have, and I want other people to talk about it too. Just getting it off of my chest, talking with you, learning about it and what it means…that all gives me hope that I can do better and feel better."

"That's great, Miranda. I'm glad our sessions are already proving valuable. From here, we're going to work on techniques to alleviate your feelings of impostor syndrome. There are a few types of methods that have been used to help with impostor syndrome. First, there's psychotherapy, which you are doing already with your therapist. Often, just having a therapist is enough for some people. They get the tools they need from working with their therapist and are able to effectively manage their impostor syndrome."

"Okay," Miranda said, wondering why her therapist referred her to Omar.

"But, other times, coaching, like you are doing with me, can prove beneficial. I've used a lot of different techniques with my clients over the years, but most recently have found that positive psychology can be effective at defeating impostor syndrome."

"Positive psychology? What's *that*?" Miranda asked.

Omar smiled, looking at his watch. "We're out of time today, but I can't wait to teach you about positive psychology in our next session. I have one request, though: please pick up a journal or blank notebook. We'll be using it a lot in our next few sessions, and I think after you learn more about positive psychology, you'll find you want to use it on a regular basis."

"Okay, I can do that. I actually have one already that will be perfect." Miranda thought of the brightly colored orange and pink notepad she received as a gift a few years ago. It would be perfect for this, and she couldn't wait to start filling it up.

That night, at around 3 am, Miranda woke up in a cold sweat. She couldn't stop thinking about the meeting she had with Tom and his boss in just a few hours. She had prepared, probably overprepared, for her plans on how to manage her new team, grow revenue, and increase employee engagement survey results. She had the data and information, and it was solid and ready to be presented, but she didn't feel ready for the meeting. She kept thinking to herself: *What if I missed something? What if Nina (the incumbent director) would have done this differently? What if Tom and his boss aren't pleased with my results?*

Miranda got up and stirred around in her kitchen, making a warm cup of milk with cinnamon. Her mind wouldn't stop spinning, anxiety consuming her. As she finished the last drop, she looked over at her colorful notepad laying on the corner of the counter. She knew right away what was happening: impostor syndrome was taking over. She couldn't wait for her next session with Omar. As she snuck back into bed, making every attempt to not wake her husband, she reminded herself that these feelings were not her fault…and she was going to defeat them.

WHAT IS POSITIVE PSYCHOLOGY?

"Omar, I cannot wait for our session today. You said you were going to teach me about positive psychology. I'm ready." Miranda screeched with excitement. She had the video chat window open on her screen and her brightly colored notepad on the desk in front of her. To her right was a hot cup of coffee. "But before we get started, I have some good news that I want to share with you, too."

"What's that?"

"Well, I was reviewing my notes from our previous sessions, and it occurred to me that I want, no, I need to build a team culture where employees are not afraid of talking about impostor syndrome. I got to thinking about how to do this and remembered how much better I felt just *learning* about impostor syndrome. So, I scheduled a meeting with human resources and proposed the idea of a voluntary group that discusses impostor syndrome."

"Wow, Miranda, that's great. What –"

Miranda interrupted. "But Omar, this was one of the hardest things I've had to do. I thought about cancelling the meeting over and over. All of these thoughts kept racing through my mind: *What if HR tells me no? Why would I be the person to lead this initiative? What if I mess up the group project so badly that it gets me fired?* And then I remembered what we talked about. I realized that so many of these thoughts were coming from impostor syndrome."

"It sure sounds like it."

"So, on the day of the meeting, despite being absolutely petrified, I walked into HR's office with sweaty palms and a racing heart. I proposed my idea."

"And what did HR say?"

"They were very receptive. At first, I wanted everyone to attend, to make it mandatory, but HR helped me to understand that our current company culture doesn't really want anyone to feel forced to do these types of things. They reminded me that sometimes talking about topics like impostor syndrome can stir up difficult emotions for people, so we agreed that we would conduct bi-weekly, voluntary, group sessions where employees can come together and talk about their impostor syndrome feelings. We're going to open it up to managers more senior than me, too, and HR will always be there, since there could be potential personnel issues."

Omar responded positively. "That's incredible. I can see how much just being able to talk about impostor syndrome has helped you, and I really like that you are giving other people the same opportunity. A group setting can be very beneficial to help with impostor syndrome."

"Yes, *and* as I learn more about positive psychology, I want to bring that information to the group sessions too." Miranda elaborated.

"Of course, that's a great idea." Omar chuckled. "Are you ready to jump in then?"

Miranda nodded.

"Okay, great. But before we get started, I want to share with you some fun facts that I just read in an article this morning. It's fitting for positive psychology, so I have to share."

Miranda nodded.

"Did you know that worrying increases cholesterol more than eating butter does?"[ix]

"What? No way." Miranda screeched, looking at her dry toast and remembering that she was up half the night worrying about the meeting with Tom and his boss today. She thought to herself, *I may as well have put butter on that toast after all…*

"I know, isn't that incredible? It's a good reminder that worrying doesn't do much for us other than harm us. Also, I learned that an optimist lives six to eight years longer than a non-optimist[ix]. Isn't that amazing?"

"Whoa, I've got to start looking at the bright side." Miranda chuckled. "You're going to help me, right, Omar? Isn't that what positive psychology is all about, being a positive person?"

"Well, that's certainly part of it. But it's more dynamic than just being positive. Positive psychology aims to help people live fulfilling lives by focusing on the things that are going well in their lives."

"Okay…" Miranda looked frustrated. Isn't living a fulfilling life basically the same thing as having a positive life, or being a positive person? And obviously, we need to focus on the good things in our lives. Miranda wanted to understand what more there was to positive psychology.

Omar chuckled. He could see the annoyance on Miranda's face. "Okay, okay, there's a lot more to it than that."

"Whew, I'm glad."

"Positive psychology is a branch of psychology founded by Martin Seligman in 1998.[ix, x, xi]. It's quite new, actually. Whereas traditional psychology focuses on what has gone wrong in one's life, the negative aspects or events, positive psychology focuses on what is going well in one's life. Its ultimate goal is to improve one's overall well-being."

"Interesting," Miranda commented. "I spend a lot of time talking with my therapist about things that have gone wrong, the bad stuff, which I have an entire life of, and it's been helpful. I wonder if this could help even more?"

"Maybe." Omar continued on. "Positive psychology wants individuals and their providers, like me, to focus on their overall well-being, not just one or two or more things that need to be improved in their lives. They take a holistic approach to helping someone find happiness and fulfillment in their life. They do this by focusing on five pillars. I can't stress this enough. It's important to remember that we are only focusing on the good things, the things that are going well in one's life. Not the bad, or the negative."

"Okay, this is really interesting. So often, I focus on what went wrong and ruminate about it over and over. I guess I'm just giving myself cholesterol problems." Miranda laughed at herself, knowing she had to stop this game of ruminating and worrying.

"Exactly, but we're going to flip the narrative. And we're going to do that by focusing on five things. In positive psychology, we call them 'the five pillars of positive psychology,' or 'PERMA.' PERMA is an acronym for:

Positive Emotions

Engagement

Relationships

Meaning

Accomplishments."

"That seems simple enough, although I have no idea how to even start practicing some of these... what did you call them? Pillars? Or PERMA?" Miranda questioned.

Omar laughed a little. "Yes, PERMA. And don't worry, that's why I'm here. Over the next few weeks, we're going to learn together more about each of these pillars, what they mean, how you can practice them, and how they can improve your life."

"Okay, but Omar, I am here, meeting with you, because you are a business leadership coach, and I need help becoming a better leader. Don't get me wrong, I'm really interested in all of this, but why are we talking about positive psychology? How is that going to help me become a better leader? Remember, I'm trying to make sure I don't disappoint Tom, or worse yet, get fired."

Miranda suddenly felt like she was wasting precious working hours sitting with Omar, talking about "happy things" and "being positive." She had reports and emails that she needed to perfect and have completed in a few days.

"You've got to trust me, Miranda. But since you asked, I want you to recall our very first session where we discussed how impostor syndrome impacts job satisfaction, career satisfaction, life satisfaction, and overall health."

"Yes, I remember…"

"Well, those same things are all impacted by someone who practices positive psychology, too. But, and this is important, the impacts are the exact opposite of how impostor syndrome impacts someone," Omar explained.

"Okay, so what you are suggesting is that someone with impostor syndrome can start practicing positive psychology and reduce their impostor syndrome?"

"That's exactly right. And Miranda, if someone's job and career satisfaction improves, aren't you doing your job as a leader?"

"Yes…" Miranda confirmed, still skeptical.

"Let's take it a step further. If an employee is less exhausted, their health improves, and their general satisfaction with life improves, aren't you doing your job as a leader above and beyond?"

"Okay, it's starting to make some sense," she confirmed.

Omar added, "*And* if all of those scales improve, don't you think that your team will perform better, bring new ideas to the table, and be more engaged? *And* improve revenue results, which is the ultimate goal, right?"

"Yes, that's a good point. So, I want to start practicing positive psychology, and I want my team to do it also. How do I get started?"

"Here are a few fun things for you to try. First, before your day ends, find someone who needs help and help them. If you see someone at the grocery struggling to get to their car with all their bags, help them. If someone can't figure out the coffee maker in the breakroom, help them."

This seemed easy enough, and Miranda made a note in her journal: help someone.

"Next, I want you to practice smiling. When I was a young boy, my mom would play the 'smile game' with my sister and me. She'd always tell us, with a big smile on her face, that she'd bet we could *not* smile for more than one minute while looking at her. You know who won, every time? Yep, that's right. Smiling is contagious, if you didn't know. It is really hard to look at someone who is smiling and not smile back. And those smiles increase endorphins, improve one's mood, and generally spread a positive ambiance. So, I challenge you to search for someone who isn't smiling and try your best to get them to crack just a little bit of a smile."

Miranda made another note: smile.

"These are two simple tasks, and I'm confident you can do these. It's really nothing more than being kind, and kindness can change someone's life *and* your life. People who practice kindness are less depressed and generally happier, and they often report receiving more kindness back in their own lives."

"Okay, I'm going to give it a try," Miranda confirmed, and she put on a big, toothy smile, somewhat jokingly, for Omar. He returned a bigger smile, and they both laughed. It really is contagious.

"I'll see you next week."

"Thanks Omar." Miranda ended the video-call and stood up. As she stretched her arms overhead, she kept a big smile on her face. She grabbed her now empty coffee cup and headed towards the breakroom. On her way, she ran into her team's lead IT manager. Still smiling, she stopped to ask how his morning was going. It was really uncomfortable for Miranda, her impostor syndrome sneaking in, but she maintained a big smile the entire time. Omar was right. After just a few seconds, they were both smiling and talking about the free donuts in the breakroom. *This could be fun,* Miranda thought to herself as she walked away, smiling and shaking her head in amazement.

When she got back to her office, she decided to send an email to her team. "Free Donuts" was the subject line. But as soon as she hit send, she started to doubt herself again. *What if there weren't enough donuts for everyone? What if someone doesn't like donuts?* Her thoughts started overpowering the goodness she was attempting to do. *Ugh, this impostor syndrome is really starting to drive me nuts!*

4

POSITIVE EMOTIONS

"Good morning, Miranda. How are you today?"

Miranda responded with a big, *big* smile on her face. She was testing him. "Omar, I'm doing well today. How about you?"

Omar returned the smile, knowing all too well that Miranda had learned something valuable: smiling is contagious.

"So, tell me, did you do your homework?"

"Yes, I did. For my act of kindness, I did a few things. First, there were free donuts in the breakroom last week. I thought it would be nice to let my team know, so I sent a group message to everyone. It felt really good at first, but then I started to doubt myself. I was afraid we would run out of donuts, or someone wouldn't like them, or someone would tell me they weren't meant for everyone."

"Okay, I see." Omar responded. "Let's talk more about those feelings in a bit. What else did you do that was kind?"

"Well, I helped my neighbor out. She just had a baby, and I can tell she's just exhausted. I saw her a few afternoons ago bringing her trash out to the curb, and could tell she was struggling with the big bin on wheels. She was wearing sweatpants, and it looked like she desperately needed a good nap and a nice shower. I had just pulled into my driveway and immediately ran over to help her. As soon as I did, I could see her feel... less alone? I'm not sure if that makes any sense, but I could feel that she needed to know that she wasn't alone."

"Wow, Miranda. What a special moment."

"I know, and it felt really good on my side. I think it meant more to me than it did to her. And really, it wasn't that big of a deal. It took just a few minutes of my time."

Omar smiled and nodded his head to the side.

"And for my smile homework, I made an effort to get every clerk or checkout person that I met this week to smile. I did it at the grocery store, at the coffee shop, and at the laundry mat. If they weren't smiling, I'd come up to them with a big smile and pay them a compliment. Things like, 'You have a beautiful shirt,' or 'I really like your hair.' It worked every time."

"That's amazing, Miranda. It sounds like you really made a difference in a few people's lives by doing just a few small gestures. I hope you can continue this practice; it's such an important concept. I also hope you can bring this into the workplace. When you think about it, we spend about a third of our lives working. Why wouldn't we want to smile while we are doing it? And of course, while we are not working."

"It's such a good point. And it's so, so easy. Now can we get started on learning about positive emotions? That's what's on the agenda for today, right?" Miranda inquired, anxious to get started.

"Yes, that's correct." Omar responded, grateful that Miranda was so receptive. "So, when we practice positive emotions, we focus only on the good emotions we experience from an event, conversation, or situation. This could be something that happened once, or it could be focusing on the positive emotions from the day, week, or month. Does that make sense?"

"Yes, we are *only* focusing on *positive* emotions or feelings."

"You got it. Here's a quick practice that is easy to implement and I believe could benefit you and others on your team. In your email inbox, create a separate email folder and label it something positive. Mine is called 'Nice Emails.' You could call it 'Positive Things' or 'I'm Amazing' or 'Great Emails.' Label it something creative and unique to you, as long as it's positive. Whenever you get a nice email from someone, a client, an employee, a vendor, even your family or friends, drag that email over to your new folder and save it there forever. Just the simple act of dragging and dropping it will light up something positive inside you. When you're having a rough day and impostor syndrome is beating you up, go to that folder and read all of the emails you've saved there. You'll be amazed at how much better you feel."

"Wow, I love that. What a fun game. I wonder how many positive emails I can save in a week or a month or even a year…"

Omar continued. "Remember, it's not a competition, just something to highlight the positive in your workday and remind you of how valuable you are."

"Got it. What else?"

"In many situations, there are good emotions and bad emotions, or positive emotions and negative emotions. Just like when you sent the email for 'Free Donuts.' You felt really good but that was also accompanied by some negative feelings of worry or shame. We want to train our minds to *only* focus on the good emotions from an event or situation. Thinking back to how you felt after you hit send on that email, tell me some of the negative feelings you had."

"I was so afraid there wouldn't be enough for everyone. I was also afraid that not everyone liked donuts. What if an employee was offended that there were no other options, or they had a meeting and couldn't get to the breakroom in time before they ran out?"

"Okay, great. Now tell me about the positive feelings you had."

"Well, I felt like the team would be very appreciative and grateful for the chance to have a free breakfast. I felt like I wasn't being greedy by withholding information that they might not have known. I also felt like I was giving the team permission to step away from their desks and take a break."

"When these situations happen, it is important to focus on the positive feelings. There will always be a way to find the negative in every situation, but there will always be a way to find the positive, too. When those negative feelings come in, I want you to stop yourself and find the positive in a situation. Put your energy into focusing on those positive emotions and pushing the negative away.

"This is a big concept. Do you want to practice some more?"

"Yes, please," Miranda confirmed.

"Okay, great. Tell me about a situation that happened recently where you just felt awful when you were done." Omar requested.

"Well..." Miranda thought for a minute.

"Oh, okay, I have something. I was in a very important meeting with a vendor just last week when Tom, my boss, asked me to present one of the slides. I wasn't prepared to present; I thought I was just going to be a bystander, but Tom sprung it on me. I didn't want to embarrass anyone, so I fumbled through the presentation. Omar, it was *awful*. I made such a fool of myself."

Miranda could feel her palms getting moist. Just talking about how poorly the presentation was made her uncomfortable and embarrassed. She felt shame overcoming her.

"Okay, that's a great example. Now, I want you to think about that meeting again, and specifically the presentation you gave unexpectedly. What were a few positive things about that presentation?" Omar asked.

"Well, I don't really know." Miranda paused. "Honestly, it was just awful."

"Okay, let's think through this together," Omar said encouragingly. "Do you consider it a compliment that Tom asked you and trusted you to present the information? He could have just done it himself, but he wanted you to do it."

"Yes, I guess that's a compliment," Miranda confirmed, hesitantly.

"Okay, let's think of another positive. What happened after the presentation?"

Miranda paused. She thought long and hard. "Well, at dinner that night with the vendor, the leader of their team and I started chatting. He told me that the information I gave him was very valuable and confirmed that they want to continue to grow our relationship. This is a really important vendor for us, so it's a big deal to keep the contract with them." Miranda started smiling proudly.

"Excellent." Omar said. "Now, focusing just on those two points that Tom *wanted* you to present and that the vendor was *happy* with your presentation, how do you feel?"

"I feel like I did a good job. But, Omar, I think I could have done better…"

"I understand, and it takes time for your mind to adjust to *only* focusing on the positive emotions, but over time, you will learn to ignore the negative emotions, like how you believe you fumbled through the presentation, or messed up by sending a message about free donuts, and you will learn to only focus on the positive emotions," Omar explained.

"Okay," Miranda said.

"Do you have another example of something that didn't go so well for you? It's important that we practice and build consistency in practicing positive emotions and we can do that together."

"Yes, I actually do, and this has been bothering me for days now. I cannot stop thinking about it. Last week, I was having a meeting with an employee who hasn't been performing very well. We had a long discussion over metrics and their performance, and towards the end of the meeting, they started sobbing. I felt terrible. Then, they told me that their mother suddenly became ill, and the prognosis isn't good. I am so mad at myself for being so insensitive."

"Okay," Omar responded. "What did you learn from this?"

"That I need to consider employees as complete humans who might also have other things going on outside of work. This employee was usually a high performer, so it makes sense now why his performance dropped so suddenly. Moving forward, I'm going to try to enter all of my employee meetings with a little more empathy."

"Wonderful, that's a great example. And I hope his mother is okay." Omar said. "So, immediately after that meeting, what could you have told yourself? Remember, only positive things."

"Okay, well…I could have told myself that I learned something that day, and to use that takeaway to make all of my employee meetings better. That's a positive that came out of the meeting. I also could have reminded myself that one of my best employees is only temporarily underperforming because of a personal issue, and that he will work on his performance so my team can flourish." Miranda stated.

"Very good," Omar said. "What you just did is called 'reframing.' Reframing is taking a situation that might lead someone to repeat negative things to themselves and to 'reframe' those thoughts into something positive, which is what we just did."

"Interesting, I like that concept." Miranda gave her validation.

"Good. Now we're going to try something else. I want you to think of the past week and tell me three things that you are grateful for. Since we're focused on your role at work, let's think of three things that you are grateful for at work, but know that you can apply this to areas outside of work too," Omar said.

"Okay, well, I am grateful for my new role, the promotion, and the new salary I received. I have a really great team. What else? Hmmm." Miranda was having a hard time coming up with things she was grateful for, especially after the intense conversations she and Omar just had.

"Oh, I know. I am grateful that HR was receptive to my ideas about starting a working group for impostor syndrome. That gets me really excited. And one more…

I am grateful for the IT department, who helped me this week when my computer system froze, and I thought I had lost the large spreadsheet I was working on. They were able to recover it in just a few hours."

"Those are wonderful things to be grateful for. When you think about how each of those events or things makes you feel, how would you describe it?" Omar asked.

"I feel really fortunate and that my hard work is paying off. It gives me some satisfaction and contentment." Miranda advised.

"Great. This is called practicing gratitude. It's quite simple, don't you think? At the end of each day, or even mid-day, ask yourself what three things you are grateful for and say them out loud. If you are able to write them down in your journal, it will reinforce those positive emotions even more. A lot of people who practice positive psychology keep a gratitude journal, just like you are. Another prompt for the journal is to answer: what went well today?"

Miranda nodded and chuckled. "Today, the update on my computer went seamlessly. I know that seems a bit mundane, but it never goes well for me, so that is something that went well today."

Miranda scribbled in her journal, making note of the success she had.

"Another really powerful exercise is to write a gratitude letter. You could do this tonight, to test it out, and see how well you feel. For this exercise, you need to think of a person who has done something for you that you appreciate… that you are grateful for. It can be someone from years ago or someone from yesterday. The timeframe isn't important. Write the letter to them, thanking them for what they've done and how it made you feel, and then ask if you can meet them in person. Don't tell them why until you see them. When you are together, tell them you want to read something to them, and then read the letter you wrote. If they interrupt, ask them to let you finish. When you are finished reading, let them express how they are feeling, and vice versa. You will both leave feeling incredible about yourselves."

Miranda smiled.

"I can tell you have someone in mind for a gratitude letter. Do you want to share?"

"Yes, a few years ago, I was going through a really difficult period in my life. I was struggling with raising a family and juggling the demands of a job. I had a big presentation, and I didn't feel I was prepared - once again. I was in the women's restroom, and the receptionist from the client's office saw me wiping tears from my face. Her name is Anne. I'll never forget. She asked why I was so emotional and listened to me. She quietly told me about the people I was going to present to and gave me some tips and tricks to help win them over. She also reminded me that having a life outside of work is okay, and it's okay to be emotional sometimes. She gave me her business card and a hug before she left. We occasionally email to stay in touch, but her advice helped me get through that presentation. I haven't seen her since, but I would love to have coffee with her. I think she deserves a gratitude letter from me."

Omar responded with a tear in his eye. "I think so too." He went on, "While it can be uncomfortable for some people at first, practicing gratitude shouldn't be difficult, and I encourage you to ask others what they are grateful for. You can do this in your team meetings or your one-on-one sessions. Hopefully, you will find that sharing your own gratitude helps to increase positive emotions, and that hearing others' gratitude increases those positive feelings even more."

"Got it. Be grateful." Miranda chuckled a little, knowing this was important, but also incredibly uncomfortable. "I think I could also express my gratitude to my team regularly, or an individual's contributions. Would that be beneficial? To express thanks to others as a way of practicing gratitude?"

"Yes, definitely. And that reinforces their positive emotions, too. Practicing gratitude can be the same as smiling, quite contagious." Omar smiled and winked. "And since we are talking about incorporating your team, do you know what else can be contagious?"

"Let me guess, reframing our mindsets?"

"That's right. Do you think you can give me an example?" Omar requested.

Miranda had been thinking about this already, so she went on to tell Omar what was on her mind. "In one of my meetings recently, an employee admitted to making an error in a programming database that caused the entire team to miss out on *a lot* of revenue. He was pretty beat up, and it was visible. No one attacked him or anything, but there was a heaviness in the room. We all moved away from the topic quickly, everyone disappointed that it would impact our bonus checks, myself included. What I could have done instead of moving off the topic was to chime in and remind the entire team that this individual, Steve, might have made an error, but that we all make errors. And the positive thing about this error was that we got rid of a client who wasn't culturally aligned with our organization. Yes, we lost some revenue, but now Steve has more time to work with new clients, who are a better fit for us, to ramp up even more revenue."

Omar nodded.

"And if I had done that, others would start to see the reframing, and eventually that would become contagious, too," Miranda said with excitement. "It also creates an environment where employees aren't afraid of sharing their missteps, which is important to me also. I want my team to be willing to share, rather than be afraid of everyone's response. I believe we can all learn from others' missteps, instead of punishing each other."

"That's exactly right. You are catching on to these concepts quite quickly. Your homework from this session is to continue thinking about how to practice positive emotions. What are you already doing? What else can you do? What about your team? What is your team already doing and what more can they do?" Omar asked her to write some ideas in her journal. "And remember, there's no scientific formula. Be creative and have fun with this."

"Omar, thank you. Thank you for being here, listening to me, and teaching me about impostor syndrome and positive psychology. Thank you for being my coach." Miranda was making every attempt to express her gratitude towards Omar, and she wanted to be intentional. Instead of just saying 'thank you,' she intentionally and genuinely told Omar what specifically she was thankful for. While it was uncomfortable, she knew it would get easier with practice and this was the first step.

5

POSITIVE ENGAGEMENT

Miranda held her first impostor syndrome working group. About half of her team showed up, more people than she expected, and HR was there to help Miranda facilitate. While Miranda was still very nervous, her own impostor syndrome feelings still rampantly appearing, she took a few minutes to explain that she was learning about impostor syndrome and what it meant. When she told the group that she, herself, was struggling with impostor syndrome, many gasped. "You don't seem like someone who has impostor syndrome."

She went on to explain how anyone can be impacted and reminded the group that no one was there to judge, but rather to share, learn, and improve together. As a leader, Miranda knew she had to help ease the uncomfortableness that often comes with being vulnerable, so she shared a few examples of how she felt when she was recently promoted.

After just a few minutes, others in the group raised their hands. They felt validated, as Miranda had hoped they would, and began sharing some of their own feelings. The HR manager smiled at

Miranda from the back of the room while taking notes about the session and how the organization could build on this in a positive way.

Towards the end of the session, one of the participants asked the same thing that Miranda had asked just a few weeks earlier with Omar: "How can we get rid of this?"

"That's why we're here," Miranda smiled. "I am learning about something called positive psychology, and I'd like to implement it into our team. I believe it will be really beneficial for us." She went on to explain to the group the little she had learned from Omar. "Who's in?" And hands went flying into the air.

"You all are wonderful. I am so grateful to have such amazing people on my team." Miranda responded. A few minutes later, she realized she was practicing gratitude, and it felt really good.

Later that week, Miranda was faced with an overwhelming amount of responsibility and numerous tasks. She was getting emails, phone calls, and people knocking at her door. She wasn't sure how she was going to get it all done, and she could hear her inner voice screaming: *You can't do this! You shouldn't have taken this job. It's too much for you. You're not going to get this work done and then they are going to fire you.*

After about an hour of composing an email, stopping to answer the phone, hanging up, then responding to someone at the door, she paused. Her colorful journal, buried under a pile of reports she needed to review, reminded her that she needed to focus on the positive. She told herself: *My employees trust me, that's why they are coming to my door. I am only getting phone calls because people need my advice, and they trust that advice. I am part of so many emails because my opinion is valued. I was put into this role because I have a lot to offer my team and this organization, and I am doing that today.*

Miranda took a deep breath and intentionally finished her emails, responded to all of her voice messages, and left the office for the day feeling grateful for a team who respected her so much.

~ ~ ~

"Omar, the impostor syndrome working group session went so well. I even had a few employees message me afterwards telling me that they felt less isolated and more connected to the team by being a part of this conversation. Isn't that so wonderful?"

"Yes, Miranda, that's great. As you recall, and you are seeing firsthand, talking about impostor syndrome is the first step to helping defeat it. I'm really proud of you."

Miranda blushed a little.

"I also met with Anne, the receptionist from years ago, and read her my gratitude letter. Omar, this was *so* uncomfortable. I almost cancelled our meeting because it just felt…weird, to read her a letter about how she helped me."

"That's totally normal, Miranda. But you did up doing it, right?"

"Yes, I did, and it was very awkward, but I read her the entire letter – a whole page and a half. When I finished, I just sat there feeling uneasy. And then Anne started to cry, and I cried because it was so emotional. I don't think either of us has cried that much in years. We ended up chatting for over an hour, about so many positive things. It felt really good. Thank you for the suggestion.

I'm going to try to do something like that once a quarter. It was an instant mood-lifter."

"That's great, Miranda. I hope you can do it again with someone else soon, and I'll be waiting to hear how it goes. Now, are you ready to learn about positive engagement?" Omar asked.

"Yes, but I don't really know what that means. It doesn't sound like it pertains to work in any way."

"Well, actually, it does, in many ways. Have you ever heard of being 'in the flow?'"

"Oh yes. That's when someone is so absorbed in an activity that they lose track of all time and forget about anything else going on around them. My son, Antonio, is 'in the flow' often, when he plays his video games late at night." Miranda says, rolling her eyes a little.

Omar laughed. "Yes, I suppose Antonio is 'in the flow' when he's playing his video games. Now let's apply that to work. Can you think of a time in the past few months where you were having so much fun with a project or task that hours went by and you forgot about other things that needed to be done?"

Miranda sat for a few minutes. She had a hard time remembering when she was last so engaged in her work that she forgot about everything else. Then it hit her. "Yes, Omar, I remember. A few months ago, I was working on a project for a client of ours. I had a giant spreadsheet open with a lot of data that had to be analyzed and then put into a PowerPoint presentation. The data had to be broken down and presented in a very simple way. Not everyone who was participating in the meeting the next day would understand the complex data. I had started the project early in the afternoon, and before I knew it, my husband was calling, asking where I was and if I was going to be home for dinner. I had worked for hours and hours on the project, but it only felt like a few minutes. I was having a lot of fun doing it, and I felt like I was doing a really good job."

"Perfect. That right there is an example of being 'in the flow.' It is a perfect example of positive engagement. When we are 'in the flow,' we are using our strengths. We can often concentrate on the task at hand with very little effort, and it often gives us energy rather than using it. Being 'in the flow' uses our innate ability and gives us enthusiasm for what we are doing. In a nutshell, when we are 'in the flow,' we are practicing positive engagement."

"Okay, yes, that makes sense." Miranda made a few notes.

"Now, we want to understand how to get *more* positive engagement for you and for your team. Right?"

"Yes, yes, we do."

"Often, individuals don't know exactly what puts them 'in the flow.' It's hard to know what being 'in the flow' feels like if someone's never experienced it, or at least consciously been aware of it. It's important to give these individuals a variety of tasks and see what intrinsically motivates them. Talk to them about their work in your one-on-one sessions and help guide them to discover what their strengths are. You could ask Tom to help you with this, too, or we can work together when you are struggling to find engagement.

For example, have you ever had an employee come to you and ask if they can work on a specific project that they might not normally be a part of? Or have you asked an employee to do a task that isn't part of their job description?"

"Yes, that happens sometimes, although not a lot." Miranda wondered to herself why people aren't coming to her if they want to work on specific projects. She started to doubt her leadership abilities again and realized her impostor syndrome was sneaking in again. *No, don't do that,* she told herself. *You are here to learn, not to doubt yourself.*

"Well, that's something we can work towards. Allowing employees to flex beyond their job descriptions and work on things that allow them to use their strengths is a big part of practicing positive engagement. We all have a different skill set, and making sure everyone's strengths are applied to the right task is important. Where this gets difficult is that, as a manager, you might not always know what an employee is interested in. This is where creating a culture of positive engagement comes into play."

"Okay, that's a great idea, Omar. But I don't think I fully understand how to do that…"

"Well, let's work on it. Have you ever wanted to be a part of a project, something that sounded really exciting, but you weren't invited to work on it?"

"Oh yes, that happened last year when we were working on a new database for our largest client. Oh gosh, I really wanted to be invited to that project team. But of course I wasn't. I was really let down, and it hurt my feelings quite a lot. I felt like I was never going to be involved in the 'fun' stuff at work."

"Well, imagine how you would have felt if you had asked to be part of the project *and* your boss allowed you to?"

"Oh gosh, that would have been so exciting for me." Miranda gazed over her computer screen and thought about how rewarding it would have been to be a part of the project team.

Omar interrupted her trance. "That is positive engagement, allowing and encouraging employees to work on tasks or projects where they feel engaged. Another way to practice positive engagement is to give employees autonomy. Now, I know that this has to be done within reason, but if we allow people to be creative and do things their own way, they become more engaged."

"That makes sense. I really dislike it when someone tells me how to do something, and the way I was doing it, or was going to do it, worked perfectly fine. That can be discouraging. But sometimes people need to work on a team, you know? Sometimes we have large projects and complete autonomy isn't possible."

"That's true, so another way to look at it is to allow that *team* to have autonomy."

Miranda made a few notes on her pad.

"It's also important to set clear and concise goals when creating autonomy. As milestones and goals are completed, immediate feedback helps to be sure that an individual is engaged in the task or project throughout its entirety, and that the work being done meets the larger organizational goals."

Miranda made another note in your journal.

"Along with this, it's also important for individuals to know that there is a growth path within their team and/or organization. Most people want to excel and advance. Most people want promotions, just like you got. They need to understand how to do that."

"Oh, well, we always have open positions in the company."

"Okay, but are you talking about them in your team meetings or one-on-one sessions? It's important for your employees to know *how* to advance, that the opportunity is there, and that you won't hold them back. Does that make sense?"

"Yes, it sure does. We have a job board where anyone can see open positions, but we don't often talk about what that means or how to grow into those roles. That's something I can work on implementing immediately. The hardest part of that, though, is that my highest performers might get promoted, and then I'll lose them."

"But think how good it will feel to know that you helped them develop and meet their own goals. Also, remember that your high performers will always want to excel. They can do that within your organization or somewhere else. It's up to you where you want them to land."

"Interesting," Miranda pondered. "I suppose if they are going to excel, it's better to keep them in the organization, although I will selfishly always want them on my team."

Omar smiled. "Of course, that's completely natural. I can see your wheels spinning already on some of the things you want to implement with your team. I promise, they'll pay off. But do me a favor? Before our next session, think about ways that *you* can also get into the flow individually. I want to hear about those times when you are working so passionately on something that your sense of time becomes distorted."

"Okay, I will, Omar. I can't wait to share what I come up with. And to learn about the next pillar of positive psychology."

A few minutes later, in her car on her way to grab a sandwich from her favorite bakery in town, Miranda found herself dancing and singing to her favorite artist. *Well, I'm definitely in the flow now,* she thought, knowing this wasn't exactly what Omar was expecting from her.

She pondered how to help her team feel more engagement and decided to start asking each of her employees at the end of their one-on-one meetings: What was the most exciting thing you worked on this week? What projects or tasks would you like to get more involved with?

She had two one-on-one meetings that afternoon, and quickly realized how important this was to her team. When Tiffany told her that she wanted to lead more meetings, Miranda asked her to take charge of that week's revenue update meeting. When William told Miranda that he was loving his part on the 'marketing ideas' team, Miranda made a note and promised William that she would keep him on that team, and also make sure he was involved in future marketing related teams.

A few days later, Miranda had her weekly one-on-one meeting with Tom. She expressed to Tom how important it was for her and her team to feel engaged, and Tom reciprocated the sentiment by asking: "Miranda, what do you need to feel engaged at work?"

Miranda couldn't answer his question immediately, but she promised him she would think about it and let him know. She knew, now, how important it was, for her, Tom, and her team to be engaged in and at work, and promised to find the project, task, or initiative that put her most 'in the flow.'

POSITIVE RELATIONSHIPS

"Today, we're going to discuss positive relationships."

"Okay," Miranda said, ready to take notes.

"Practicing positive relationships means that an individual needs to have a person or persons in their life, or in this case, at work, who help them feel supported. We want an individual to have someone at work that they can trust, and who they can share the good things happening in their job…and also the things that might not be going so well (even though that sounds contrary to positive psychology principles). You may have seen the question on employee engagement surveys: Do you have a best friend at work? There's a reason for this. Individuals who have a 'best friend' at work are less likely to be searching for another job."

"Interesting. I don't have any friends at work," Miranda stated, sadly.

"Are you sure, Miranda? You've mentioned a woman named Ginnie that you have lunch with sometimes."

"Oh yes, I guess Ginnie is a friend. I met her a few years ago when my team was collaborating with her team. We had a lot of fun, and a lot of the same frustrations, and started going to lunch every day. I guess you're right. Ginnie is a friend I have at work."

"That's great," Omar said. "Even though they often are, a positive relationship at work doesn't always have to mean a 'friendship.' Rather, it just means having people in the workplace that consistently bring you up, listen to you, support you, and help you to further your career…and ultimately your life."

"That makes sense."

"But we also want to talk about *how* we can build those positive relationships, both individually and as a team, right? It all seems great in theory, but what does it look like? It's not always easy to make friends, especially in such a formal setting."

"Yes, that's a good point. For Ginnie and me, it just kind of happened… organically. But I suppose not everyone is able to so naturally create positive relationships. So, Omar, how do I, or we (my team), begin practicing positive relationships?"

"Well, it's important to remember that positive relationships are more than just having a relationship with someone. It's about how we communicate and support each other. We don't have to be 'friends' to do that. And as a leader, director now, you need to lead by example, especially if you want to build a culture of positive psychology."

"Right." While it was starting to settle with her that Miranda was finally a director, every time someone reminded her, she had a sudden wave of fear rush through her. *I am the director now. I have to be a leader,* she reminded herself.

"This starts not just with your words, but with your body language too. Do you always close your office door? Are you always cheerful with people? What's your tone of voice like?"

"That makes sense. My demeanor can influence my relationships." Miranda's very introverted tendencies caused her to close her door often. This had to change, and she knew it.

"Absolutely. And that includes conflicts, too. You don't strike me as someone who raises their voice or gets visibly upset when things go wrong. Is that true?"

"Yes, I tend to pout to myself instead." She didn't really know how else to cope with conflicts at work.

"Well, remember that it's important to discuss those frustrating situations with the parties involved. Pouting about it doesn't change anything. But discussing it shows maturity, responsibility, and an example for others on how to address conflict with their peers. It's exactly like you mentioned a few sessions ago when Steve made an error that cost the team their bonuses. Talking about it creates and builds positive relationships."

"It's also kind of like when I fight with my husband. Antonio (my son) sees *how* we fight and learns those skills. He mirrors them at school, with his friends, and with his father and me, so modeling healthy emotional regulation is important."

"Yes, exactly. That applies to conflicts that might happen with Tom or others in a more senior position than you, too. Even if

59

they are upset, demeaning, or not handling the situation well, you have the power to control yourself. If you are able to healthily resolve the conflict, you will feel more capable than you realize."

"That makes a lot of sense, and it's less intimidating. I know that when a boss, senior leader, or even a peer gets really upset with me, I often shut down and am unable to finish my work effectively. I'm open to constructive feedback, but yelling and putting me down are not effective."

"That is very true. Much of practicing positive relationships starts with how we communicate with each other. Let's touch on another part of communicating that's so important. Think of a conversation you might have had recently in the workplace, maybe one that didn't end with you feeling so great about the event."

"Okay, well, how about that same conversation I had with the employee whose mother is ill?"

"Perfect. You learned about reframing in that conversation, which helps positive emotions. How could you have communicated more effectively in that conversation? Obviously, it's over, and hindsight is always 20/20, but let's use it as an example and learning opportunity."

"Well, I could have been more patient with him. As soon as he told me about his mother, I could have just stopped any conversation about his performance and listened to him. I once had a very ill mother, before she passed away, and I know how important and comforting it was for me to just talk about it. I could have told him that we would schedule another time to discuss his performance and asked if there was anything the team or I could do for him or his family."

"Very good. Would you say that all of that encompasses being empathetic?"

"Yes, I suppose it does."

"Empathy is so important in communication...and in practicing positive relationships. Having empathy and allowing people to talk without veering them away from a topic solidifies trust, and building trust builds relationships. A great way to do this is to ask open-ended questions...and to be genuine about it. Listen actively and give people the chance to talk."

"That's true..."

"Another way to help build trust in relationships is to be transparent with individuals and/or your team. For example, if there is a big change happening at the company, being as transparent as possible can help build trust. You appreciate when Tom shares information with you, right?"

"Yes, I do. It helps me to know that I am doing the right thing and what my future with the company looks like."

"Exactly. And that also means communicating when things don't go as planned. Transparency doesn't always mean sharing the good things; it means sharing the bad stuff too. And yes, I know we are here to talk about positive things, but in this case, sharing the negative stuff helps to build trust. We're all adults and know that life doesn't always go as planned, that we all make mistakes, and that we are all in this together.

Trust is so important in all aspects of our lives. We need to trust each other, and as a role model, you can do that by being predictable. Make sure your team is never afraid to approach you and that when there is something to share, you share it, assuming you are permitted to do so. If some things are shared, and not others, or some days you are grumpy and other days skipping and jumping with a big smile, an employee will never know what to expect, and that decreases their trust."

"I understand," Miranda said.

"And Miranda, here's the most important one: you have to learn to trust yourself."

Miranda looked down in shame.

"When an employee sees that you trust yourself, they learn to trust themselves. And then they learn to trust each other. You are the role model now. Trust yourself."

"I'm working on it, Omar, but it's really hard."

"I know. It's part of impostor syndrome, and we'll continue working on it together. Can you think of a recent situation where you would have benefited from trusting yourself?"

"Hmmm…" Miranda thought for a few minutes. She had so many scenarios, and many recent, where she knew she was as trusting of herself as she could be.

"Last week, I had a meeting with one of our vendors. I wasn't sure if I should bring up the concerns we were having with one of their products, which was creating some pain for my entire team. For the first half of the meeting, I went back and forth on the topic in my mind. I was quietly messaging a few others from my phone, asking if I should bring up the issue, and of course, I was distracted from the content being presented. In the end, I brought up the problem, and a resolution was made. It was a win-win. But looking back on it, had I trusted myself from the beginning, I wouldn't have been teetering all over the place, unfocused on the rest of the meeting. I should have just trusted myself. And I can see now how doing that would have built more respect with all of the other people I was messaging during an important meeting. They must have thought I was *crazy*."

Omar chuckled. "I doubt they thought you were crazy, but this is a perfect example. Remember this next time you are in doubt. Trust yourself. Also, how could you reframe that, using lessons from positive emotions?"

"Oh, that's a good point. I didn't say anything positive about that situation." Miranda kicked herself. She wanted to do better at practicing positive psychology, but her old habits got in the way. *Man, this is hard,* she thought. *But I'm going to keep persisting forward.*

"Instead of saying that everyone must have thought I was crazy, I could have reframed it to say that 'everyone must have thought I was so passionate about the problem and really wanted a strong resolution.' I could have also quietly told myself that same message, which would have helped me to build my own trust."

"You got it," Omar confirmed. "And here we are, already merging multiple pillars of positive psychology to help you improve."

Miranda smiled and inquired further. "How can I build positive relationships when it comes to doing task-oriented work? We talked about building positive relationships if an employee has a personal issue or if the larger organization has something going on, but what about specific work-related relationships? You know, the day-to-day relationships?"

"Great question. My advice is to be as open and receptive to ideas as you can be. Your team, I'm sure, has a lot of ideas on how to complete the same shared goals. Give them permission to express those, allow them to try them, and encourage diverse perspectives. You've already told me about your team dynamic, and with the varying cultures and ethnicities in your group, you are bound to receive a wide array of thoughts and ideas. This can be difficult, but you want to avoid any negative talk in the group and be sure the rhetoric is always changed to inclusivity and creativity. As your team starts to realize that they won't be penalized or mocked for an idea, they will eventually start to bring more and more to the table. And this will help your team, don't you think?"

"Yes, you are probably right. And I always want everyone to feel welcome. What I am hearing you say is that to practice positive relationships, I need to practice inclusivity and create a welcoming culture?"

Omar nodded.

"Okay, anything else?" Miranda asked.

"Well, remember, Miranda, there's no prescription or map to building any of these five pillars. These are just ideas and suggestions. You can be creative and find what works for you and your team. I encourage you to do this. Build off of what we are discussing and make it your own."

Miranda smiled and nodded.

"I encourage you to allot time in each employee's workday - and yours too, for personal connection. If you see employees gathered in the coffee room chatting, give them space to bond. Encourage your team to gather together for lunch. Build in a few minutes during meetings for people to connect. And you should do this, too, and become part of those conversations. You might be their boss, but you are a human being just like them."

"That's true, I am."

"You can design team events during or after work hours if it feels culturally appropriate for your organization, but remember that not everyone enjoys large group activities. You don't want to push this too much because it could have the opposite effect for someone who prefers a more one-on-one or smaller group setting."

"Yes, I am one of those people, a little more introverted, so I can understand how that could be a turnoff for some people. But I do like the idea of cultivating conversations with colleagues throughout the day. I also think that those informal conversations can create some of the best ideas."

"For sure. When there is less pressure to perform or create, people can be more relaxed. You are on to something."

Miranda reviewed her notes. She was feeling overwhelmed but also really hopeful that all her sessions with Omar would pay off.

"How are you feeling, Miranda? We've gone over three of the five pillars."

"I'm feeling a bit overwhelmed with the immense amount of information you've given me, but it's all great material, Omar. I think I'll be ready to tackle the fourth pillar in our next session." Miranda said.

"Great, I'm so glad."

"Oh, one more thing. I forgot to tell you about how I am going to work on positive engagement, the topic we talked about in our last session. I've thought about this a lot, and it was really difficult, but when Tom was out on vacation a few weeks ago, I had to jump in on a project he was working on with the marketing team. I found it to be really engaging. So much so that I completely forgot about lunch. Well, just two days ago, and after I had my one-on-one session with Tom where he asked what put me in the flow, I realized that I needed to ask Tom if I could be involved in more projects like that. Do you know what he said?"

"What?" Omar raised his eyebrows.

"He asked me if I wanted to take the lead on it. He told me that it was one of his least favorite tasks to work on, and he would be happy to have it off his plate, especially if it got me in the flow. So, now it's mine. Isn't that great?"

"Yes, it sure is. A real win-win. Positive psychology is working already, and it's helping you to defeat your impostor syndrome. Having the opportunity to upskill and grow is an important part of positive engagement and positive psychology in general. I'm so glad you had this opportunity. You are doing wonderfully in our sessions, but we still have more to learn, so until next time, think about how you can practice positive relationships."

The next morning, as Miranda rushed into her office after getting stuck in traffic for 30 minutes, she kicked her office door shut behind her. She sat down in a frenzy, took a deep breath, and stood back up. She walked to the door, opened it calmly, and smiled as she sat back down at her desk. Her demeanor was important, and rushing in and kicking doors shut was not how she wanted to lead.

Later, as she was warming her bagel in the toaster, a group of young employees came in from her team. She had overhead them chatting about a party they had been at the weekend before. As soon as they saw her, they became silent. Miranda smiled big and asked them if they are all friends outside of work. One of the young men smiled and said, "Yes, we all became friends here and now we have barbeques every Thursday after work."

Miranda told them that it was wonderful to see them bonding and that she was so happy they had formed a strong friendship. They all chatted for another 20 minutes or so, Miranda included, about their favorite barbeque dishes. When Miranda left, the young group was still congregated in the break room, and she smiled and nodded in encouragement. As she turned the corner and started down the hallway, she overhead one of the young women begin to ask, "Do you think that project we are working on would benefit…" She couldn't hear their conversation the further away she got, but was grateful that warming her bagel that morning led to team bonding, ideas, and something positive.

POSITIVE MEANING

"Good morning, Miranda. How are you today?"

"Hi Omar. I'm doing really well."

"Wonderful. Let's jump right in. Can you tell me how practicing positive relationships is going? Have you had a chance to practice this pillar?"

"Well, it's going alright. We had another impostor syndrome working group, and I started thinking that the group is already practicing positive relationships, even though we haven't talked about it. There's connection, empathy, and listening in that group. Since it's an in-office meeting, I started thinking about our remote workers from other offices. I wanted them to be included, so I set up video conferencing software in the conference room and extended the invite to all remote workers. So now we have even more people in our working group. It's been a really productive group. We're still learning and talking about impostor syndrome, but I'm hoping in our next session we can start to discuss positive psychology."

"Oh, Miranda, that's wonderful to hear. And yes, you are building positive relationships in that group, and I'm so happy to hear that you thought of the remote workers. We're living in a new time where we need to consider each of them too, and this is a great start to making sure they become a part of the positive psychology culture you are building. But what about the people on your team who aren't part of that group, either in-office or remote? Have you had a chance to practice positive relationships with any of them? Or maybe a relationship outside of your team that benefits you?"

"Yes, I am also working on practicing positive relationships individually. For example, when I begin each meeting, whether it's with an individual or a group, I do a check-in. I ask how everyone is doing, and then I listen with intent. I've found that listening to people without worrying or thinking about what I'm going to say next has given me insight into who each person is and what drives them. A few people will talk and talk and talk, but I'm learning about what motivates and empowers different people, and it gives me so many ideas to better the team."

"Like what?"

"Well, for one, succession planning. I know who can step in on various projects if they need to. I'm also learning about the team's different interests, and it helps me when thinking about new projects coming up and who can be assigned to various tasks. But you know what, Omar?"

"What?"

"I'm really feeling a connection to my team, like they are more than employees, they are people, and I want the best for them.

And I'm feeling like they want the same for me. I'm trying to share more about my interests and goals at work, and the team seems to be creating a new level of respect for me that I didn't understand or think existed. It's been a really positive change, just focusing on being present, empathetic, and aware of my work relationships."

"A positive change? No pun intended, right?" Omar smiled and winked.

Miranda laughed at her own slip-up.

"Okay, well, keep practicing your positive relationships and emotions and engagement, too. Reinforcement will only make it become more and more natural, for both you and the culture of your team. Today, let's dig into practicing positive meaning."

Miranda readjusted herself on the chair she was sitting on. She had no idea what positive meaning was, and Omar could see the hesitation and confusion on her face.

"Positive meaning is when people feel that they have a larger purpose in their communities and in the world as a whole. People who are good at practicing positive meaning feel that they have a purpose larger than just themselves." Omar explained.

Miranda nodded. This sounded like a big concept, and a hard one to achieve.

"That's a pretty basic definition of positive meaning. But given that brief explanation, how could you translate that to the workplace? How do you think someone who practices positive meaning in the workplace feels or behaves?"

Miranda was silent for quite some time. She took a sip of coffee, made a scribble on her notepad so Omar would think she was taking notes, even though she was just confused. Finally, she admitted that she had no idea how this could apply to the workplace.

"Honestly, Omar, I don't see how someone having a bigger purpose can apply to the workplace. I can understand how religion, or community service, or philanthropic efforts might give someone purpose. Even having a family or a close group of friends can give someone meaning, but I'm not connecting the dots to how this applies to work."

"Okay, I can see how it's a bit confusing. Let me put it another way. In the workplace, someone who practices positive meaning understands that the work they are doing contributes to more than just their role, their team, and their organization. They understand that their role – big or small – has a larger purpose in society."

Miranda was still stumped and getting frustrated. "Omar, I have no idea what this looks like or how to apply it."

"Okay, think of your community. Who does your organization serve?" Omar responded patiently.

"Well, in my community, we serve a few banks, the larger supermarket chain, and dozens of restaurants, to name a few."

She paused. "Okay, I think I'm starting to understand it. Our work impacts the community. So the work that one employee does impacts the team, which impacts the organization, which impacts the community. I've never thought of it that way."

"That's correct. Now, there are a few ways to help increase positive meaning. If I ask you, *why does your work matter?* How would you respond?"

"I would tell you that being a good leader helps my team to be successful. And a successful team means we have more revenue and more money to give for annual pay increases and bonuses, for example. There are lots of benefits to having a successful team. But having higher revenue means that my team can bring home larger paychecks, and that might mean that they can send their kids to college, or put a down payment on a home, or, well, whatever they want to do. In a nutshell, being a successful leader means giving a better life to the team I am leading."

"That's great. Now, how does your work impact your community?"

"Well, if my team wasn't successful, the businesses in our community wouldn't be able to operate, or at least not the way they are now. That could mean that some people in the community could lose their jobs. So I guess that 'my work matters' because it helps to keep a thriving community." Miranda said. "I need to remind myself of this every morning before I start working."

"That's a great idea, Miranda. You could even put a sticky note on your computer reminding yourself of why your work is important and what the purpose of your work is. And writing it down will reinforce it. You could include a 'meaning and purpose' section in your journal if you find that writing it down helps you."

"That's a great idea."

"As you practice positive meaning with your team, it's important to always remember the larger picture. When a person or persons become frustrated with a project or task, we need to slow down a little and ask them how this impacts the entire organization, their community, and, if applicable, humanity as a whole. Sometimes, as humans, we can get caught up in the mundane pieces of a long-term goal, often forgetting the purpose of the task at hand. How we address those and frame the situation can really drive positive meaning, even with the most difficult or boring tasks."

"That makes sense - to never lose sight of the *real* purpose of our work."

"Exactly."

"I know we need to end this session a little early so you can make it to your son's soccer game. How are you feeling, though?"

"Well, to be honest, Omar, this session feels a bit more difficult to implement in the real world. I'm going to spend some time reflecting on it, but I might want to discuss it further in one of our future sessions."

"That's no problem, Miranda. It's why I'm here. In the meantime, do this for me: spend some time brainstorming on other ways you might be able to practice positive meaning, and let's discuss them in our next session. Cool?"

"Of course. Thanks, Omar."

As Miranda watched Antonio kick the black and white soccer ball across the field, she reflected on her session with Omar. When she started to think about the things that mattered most in her life, the first things to come to mind were personal: her family, her friends, her health. She really pondered how her work mattered, but also knew that she was incredibly grateful for her career.

Antonio kicked the ball hard and made a goal. Miranda stood up and cheered, "Go Antonio!" He waved back at her, and his bright red shoes stood out on the green grass. She had just purchased them for him; something he had been wanting for years. It felt really good that she was able to do it for him, and it was largely because of her new promotion.

In this moment, what mattered was her ability to give her son a better life, and that happened because of her career. It was small, she knew that, but by giving Antonio a good life with abundant opportunities, and by being a good parent, she was helping to build the next generation of humanity.

That night, in her journal, Miranda flipped to a blank page and wrote 'Meaning' at the top of the page. On the next few lines, she wrote:

Being a good parent so I can help to give the next generation opportunities.

Being a good leader so I can help my team and their families to have opportunities.

Building a positive psychology culture so my team and I can enhance our well-being.

Miranda went to bed that night pondering the role she played in her personal life, her work life, and in the world. She knew it was much bigger than she ever thought, and wanted her team to understand this about themselves, too.

POSITIVE ACCOMPLISHMENTS

"I've spent some time brainstorming and making all sorts of random notes about how I can implement positive meaning at work."

"Okay, great. Let's talk about them. But first, how did Antonio do in the soccer game?"

"Oh, thanks for asking. His team won, 2-0."

"Oh, great. I'm so happy to hear. Okay, now tell me what you've come up with for positive meaning?"

"I've only got two solid ideas, but it's a start. I know this will be a work-in-progress and new ideas will always come to me, but tell me what you think of these. First, I was thinking about the sticky note, which I have on my computer now, that says: Why does my work matter? I read it every morning, and it reminds me that I am here for more than just me or my immediate team. It feels good. And then I started thinking that I need to ask myself the same question at the end of the day, too. I'm starting to create a habit that when I shut down my computer each day, I quietly ask myself: What did I do today that mattered? It's been helping me to close out my day on a positive note, and I leave feeling like I've done good for the world."

"That's amazing, Miranda. Keep up that great work. You said there was a second idea you had?"

"Yes, I think it's important for my team to know that having a purpose in their community is important. I'm considering asking HR if we could take a half day each quarter to do something for the community. We could volunteer at the food bank, plant trees, or do anything that the team really feels passionate about. I think it's important for them to know that coming to work each day is about more than just which tasks they are assigned, and this could help with relationship building also. It sort of kills two birds with one stone."

Omar smiled and responded. "You've got some great ideas. I love how intertwined the different pillars of positive psychology are becoming. You'll soon see that in almost all situations, more than one pillar of positive psychology can be implemented, and often without even trying or knowing it. I'm so happy you are thinking outside the box and can't wait to see how these ideas continue to progress. Congratulations on your work so far."

"Thanks, Omar." Miranda blushed.

"That's a great segway to our final pillar: positive accomplishments. Do you have ideas about what this might mean?"

"Sure, I think it means celebrating when we accomplish something big," Miranda exclaimed.

"Yes, that's part of," Omar smiled at Miranda's excitement. "Let me elaborate on that thought, though. Think about the goal that Tom and the organization set for you a few years ago, where you had to grow your client base by 100 new clients each year. You get excited when you meet that goal, right?"

"Yes, absolutely."

"An important part of making sure goals are achievable, so you feel good about them, is to be sure you are setting SMART goals.[ix]"

"SMART goals? Aren't all goals *smart?*"

Omar chuckled. "It's an acronym: SMART. It stands for:

Specific

Measurable

Achievable

Relevant

Time-bound

Let's dig into each of these a bit more."

"Okay."

"Starting with **specific**. A goal needs to be clear and unambiguous. There need to be no questions about what the goal is, how it will be accomplished, or who will accomplish it. Let's use the example of getting new clients. If Tom had told you he wanted you to grow the team revenue, is that clear?"

"Well, kind of, but not really. I wouldn't know how much, or how, or what the deadline is."

"Exactly. A SMART goal needs to be very clear and specific. Next is **measurable**. For this goal, it's easy to measure. Your goal is to get 100 clients. If you get 75, you can measure it. If Tom said, 'Get new clients by the end of the year,' you cannot measure your progress because you don't know what the final goal, the number of clients, is."

"That makes sense. Next is **achievable**?"

"Yes, for a goal to be **achievable**, it needs to be realistic. If Tom asked you to get one million new clients, it's not attainable. You would just give up on such an unrealistic goal. All goals need to be realistic, attainable, and thus, achievable.

Relevant is next. A goal needs to make sense. It needs to align with the long-term goals of the larger organization, or even an individual's long-term growth. For example, you are trying to improve impostor syndrome, and that's relevant because you want to be a better leader in your new role. But in the case of new clients, it's relevant because new clients are what help the organization to grow. If Tom set a goal of, let's say, learning to successfully change a tire by the end of the month, you would be so confused. It's not relevant to your role at work or anything your organization does. That's a bit extreme, but I hope it helps you to understand how relevance is important."

"Yes, it makes sense."

"And finally, **time-bound**. Goals need to have a timeline. Tom has requested you to get 100 new clients by the end of the year. You know you have ten months left in the year, so that's ten new clients a month. It's time-based and gives you a deadline. Instead of procrastinating, you have an objective timeline to follow.

Each of these components in a SMART goal is important for accomplishing goals. It's important for individuals to set SMART goals at work, and individually, to feel accomplishment when they are finished."

"Wow, I never knew any of this. I feel so uninformed. I think some of this is already happening naturally in our yearly objectives, but I want to make sure my team and I all have SMART goals in place."

"Now, think about a goal that you set for yourself, maybe your goal of improving impostor syndrome and positive psychology with your new team. If you accomplish that goal, you'll be excited too, right?"

"Yes, of course, I'd be thrilled."

"Now, both of those goals, new clients and improving impostor syndrome and positive psychology, bring excitement. You'll celebrate both accomplishments, but when you think of the emotions that come with each, how do they differ?"

"Well, for me, impostor syndrome and positive psychology are much more personal, and accomplishing those goals would be more meaningful to me. I would still be really happy about the goal of new clients too, but I understand what you are suggesting: the feelings are different."

"Exactly. Part of positive accomplishments is setting goals that are achievable and congruent to our own goals."

Miranda nodded. She knew her organization set goals for each team and each person's job description, but she wanted to learn what else her team and each individual employee wanted to accomplish. She made a note of this.

"And now is the fun part: celebrating those accomplishments. In life and work, there are always going to be misses, or goals that aren't met. But when those goals *are* met, when something has been accomplished, it is important that we acknowledge it. I want to talk about the feedback we give to each other when we accomplish a goal."

"Okay."

"There are four ways of giving feedback. They are:

Active-Constructive

Passive-Constructive

Active-Destructive

Passive-Destructive

"With **active-constructive** feedback, the person giving the feedback is excited and engaged in the feedback, making it positive and inquiring more about the accomplishment. Let's use the same example we've been on. Let's say you achieved the goal of getting 100 new clients and went to Tom to tell him. Active-constructive feedback would sound something like 'Congratulations, Miranda. Who was the final client? How did you win them over? How did you feel when they signed the final contract? I can't wait to share this information with the board. We're going to beat all of our revenue goals.'

"With **passive-constructive** feedback, the person giving the feedback is supportive but quiet. They don't engage and ask for further details, but they don't make the feedback negative either. In this example, Tom might just simply say 'Congratulations.'"

"Okay, I can see the difference here."

"Yes, how we respond is so important. In **active-destructive** feedback, the person giving the feedback is engaged but also critical, pointing out the negatives of the accomplishment. In this type of feedback, Tom might say, 'That's great, Miranda, but how are we going to staff for this? We weren't expecting you to meet this goal for another two months, so this will be a challenge for the team.'

And finally, in **passive-destructive** feedback, the person giving the feedback is passive and not interested in the accomplishment at all. For example, Tom might say, 'Okay, when will you have your monthly financial report for me?' In this case, he hardly acknowledges what you have told him and is more concerned about something else unrelated to the achievement. You can see how this is incredibly discouraging and destructive."

"Yes, that's awful. Tom is never quite that passive. I'm grateful for that."

"The way we give feedback is important. This is another opportunity for you to be a role model and a leader. As you now know, a culture of positive psychology can start with just one person. Now, tell me, Miranda, when you achieve something you've been working on, how do you celebrate that accomplishment?"

"Well, I might go out for a nice dinner with my husband or son. Or I might buy myself something I've wanted for a while, like a new sweater or piece of jewelry."

"That's great. And you do that after the goal has been accomplished, right?"

"Yes, of course, I wouldn't want to celebrate before the goal is complete."

"Okay, so let's focus on your goal of obtaining 100 new clients in a year. If you only celebrate once you have contracts for 100 new clients, you only get to celebrate once a year. But what if you and your team have 53 new clients in April already? You've now achieved more than half of your goal and there's still eight months left in the year. Isn't that something to be proud of?"

"Okay, okay. I see. Celebrating an accomplishment is about more than the big ending. It's important to celebrate the milestones along the way."

Omar smiled and nodded.

"Exactly. This is true of our careers also, in a much larger sense. We all need to celebrate and be confident in what we have accomplished in our careers so far, even if it's not the job we are striving for. It takes time to get the perfect job, at the perfect company, with the perfect boss. But in the meantime, the work we are doing is helping us attain that bigger goal, and we need to be proud of it.

So often, as humans, we only celebrate when we get to the big ending. But creating a culture of smaller milestones is important. You can do this by breaking a bigger project or an annual goal into smaller milestones. Let's use that same goal of obtaining 100 new clients. Perhaps your team could celebrate, and make it known beforehand what the celebration milestones are, when you get to 10% of the clients, or 30%, or when a well-sought-after client is brought on board."

"That's a great idea."

"To help hold everyone accountable, it's important to track the progress publicly. For example, in team meetings, you could have a few minutes to show a dashboard of current results and use team shout-outs to celebrate goal accomplishments. It's important to include the entire team in these moments of celebrating and give everyone a chance to acknowledge their own success or someone else's. It's likely that someone might have something positive to share that you aren't aware of. Let everyone be a part of practicing accomplishments, big or small."

Miranda was vigorously taking notes.

"In addition, it is important to celebrate accomplishments such as new ideas, creative thought processes, or an individual's completion of a new certificate, for example. Remember to celebrate as much as you can, not just when a measurable outcome has been completed. If you can find something to celebrate every day, that's even better, even if it's just a self-congratulation to yourself. For example, today I completed my 50th gym visit this year. I know that's not work-related, and not many other people will care all too much, but I'm proud of myself, and I'll write it in my journal this evening."

"That's great. I can see how finding something small to celebrate each day can build positivity. By the way, congrats on the gym visits. Even if you don't tell anyone else, I am happy for you."

Omar blushed. Miranda's hand was starting to hurt. She had so many notes and great ideas.

"Also, like many of our other positive psychology practices, writing down accomplishments can reinforce positivity. Keep a personal reflection section in your journal and write down those frequent accomplishments. Or ask your team to send their accomplishments each week and share them with the group (if they are appropriate).

You could go as far as to have a wall or area in the office where your team can write things they are proud of or recently accomplished, or encourage handwritten notes congratulating each other. There are so many different ways to celebrate, and sometimes the littlest of gestures is just as meaningful as an expensive award."

Omar took a big sigh. "That's a lot of information."

"It is. I love these ideas, though. I can't wait to share these with my team and ask about something everyone accomplished that week in our next team meeting. And then, to celebrate."

"That's fantastic, Miranda. What do you think you will share as an accomplishment with your team in your next team meeting?"

"Well, Omar, we just finished learning about the last pillar of positive psychology. I have a wealth of new information, and I want to celebrate that with my team."

Both Miranda and Omar smiled widely. "I can't wait to hear about it in our next session, Miranda."

Miranda disconnected the video-call and immediately pulled up the slides for her regular team meeting. She had a format for her meetings, with a pattern of slides that was consistent from meeting to meeting. Now, she added a slide at the end with the title 'Celebrating Accomplishments.' She started by listing the team objectives and how close each of them were to being met. Her team was making really nice progress this year, and it was so rewarding to see it shown on her screen. She had a feeling that the team was unaware of all they had achieved, and by seeing the results, it would bring them some positive momentum to keep striving forward.

She also added a section for other achievements. She knew a few team members had participated in the recent certification course and completed it successfully. She wanted to congratulate them and celebrate together with the team. Finally, she added a question at the end of the slide: What is everyone celebrating this week?

Miranda couldn't wait for her team meeting in two days. She was feeling so connected, engaged, confident, and authentic as a leader.

Does Positive Psychology Really Help Impostor Syndrome?

"Good afternoon, Miranda. How are you today?"

"I'm doing really well. I'm so excited to tell you about my most recent experiences."

"Great, I can't wait to hear about them. And celebrate them." Omar winked.

"Well, as you know, I've been working with you once a week for eight weeks. Can you believe we've been doing this for two months? Anyway, that's not the important part. The point is that it's been two months since I received my promotion. Things are going really well with the team, but last week an employee, Sasha, came into my office and asked if we could talk. Sasha explained to me that she was struggling with a client of hers, and it was really impacting her life, both at work and at home. She expressed how stressed she was, and I could see that she was visibly upset."

Omar leaned his head to the side, listening intently.

"I reminded myself of the importance of listening with empathy. Sasha expressed how one of the employees at the client's office was degrading and hurtful, even when the business was going well. I expressed to Sasha that it was not okay to be treated that way, and I could tell she felt validated. Her shoulders started to relax, and I could sense that we were building trust."

"That's great." Omar validated, waiting for a resolution to the story.

"I asked Sasha why she thought the employee was so hateful, and she told me that with the restructuring that happened six months ago, the organization reassigned certain clients to new account managers. This particular client really enjoyed working with Daniel. She thinks that the client is upset that they can't work with Daniel anymore. And then Sasha went on to explain how it makes her feel like she's not good at her job, like her other clients are going to get upset, and that someone might fire her."

"Okay…"

"We talked about how we could resolve the situation, and Sasha said that it would be best for Daniel to take the client back. She expressed that she didn't really like the client's mission, anyway, and that some of their operations went against her own ethics. I told Sasha that if Daniel takes the client back, she might have to take one or two of his clients to balance the workload, and she was okay with that. I told her I would talk with Daniel and get back to her.

"A few days later, after I had a conversation with Daniel, I pulled Sasha back into my office. I reminded Sasha that the relationship with the client had nothing to do with her and that they just missed working with Daniel. I asked her to repeat it out loud to me to reinforce the positive thinking: 'The client did not have an issue with me; they just missed the relationship they had with Daniel. All of my other clients love my work.' Then I told her that Daniel also missed working with that client and he was glad to have them back."

Omar smiled.

"I could see the relief on Sasha's face. I felt so good about being able to help her in a positive way. A few days later, I received a message from Sasha thanking me for being so receptive to her challenges. She told me that she had been considering looking for a new job, but because we were able to work together, she decided to stay. At the end of the message, she asked if we could set up our next team at a local nursing home. They are one of her clients, but her grandmother also lives there, and she knows how important it is for the residents there to have visitors. Of course, I told her yes and thanked her for transparency and honesty. In our next team meeting, I asked the group what everyone was celebrating that week, and Sasha chimed in: 'This week, I am celebrating how well I was able to handle a difficult situation with a client. I was so afraid I wouldn't be able to find a resolution, but together with Miranda, we turned a difficult situation into a win-win.'"

Omar applauded quietly but visibly while smiling.

"After that team meeting, I felt like I was on top of the world. I went into my office and pulled out my positive psychology journal. Under positive emotions, I wrote:

Today, I am grateful for Omar, learning about positive psychology, and having the ability to implement my new skills with my amazing team.

"Under positive engagement, I wrote:

Today, I felt like I was in the flow while I helped Sasha and Daniel find clients that aligned with their needs, desires, and skillsets.

"Under positive relationships, I wrote:

This week, I fostered a relationship with Sasha that built trust. I am confident that the next time she is struggling with something, she will come to me quicker and with less hesitation.

"Under positive meaning, specifically *What did I do today that mattered?* I wrote:

Today, I changed Sasha's life and received praise for it. I might have also saved a client. But most importantly, I gave Sasha the relief she needed while thinking creatively about how to do it.

"Under positive accomplishment, I wrote:

Today, I watched Sasha celebrate her fear of coming to me with a concern. The entire team celebrated. I know that my new training in positive psychology is helping not just me, but my entire team. To celebrate, I am going to get the expensive ice cream from the supermarket and bring it home for ice cream sundaes.

"And then I got to thinking that I needed these prompts visible for me every day. I created a large poster and hung it on the wall beside me, so I could see it each day. It says:

Have I practiced positive psychology today?

- Positive Emotions

    - What am I grateful for today?

    - What are three things that went well today?

- Engagement

    - When did I feel in the flow today?

    - What strength did I use today?

- Relationships

    - Who did I connect with today?

    - What kind thing did I do for someone else today?

- Meaning

    - What did I do today that mattered?

    - What did I do today that contributed to something larger than myself?

- Accomplishments

    - What progress or achievement am I proud of today?

○   What did I celebrate today and how?

"Each morning, I look at it and remind myself, quickly, of what each pillar stands for. If I need a refresher, I pull up our notes. One of the best parts about what I've learned from you is coming into work and starting my day off on a positive note. And a few days ago, I saw that the team was also creating their own versions of positive psychology reminders. A few of them had PERMA posters on their cubicle walls. I think it's the beginning of a cultural shift, and I'm so happy about it."

Miranda stopped talking, took a deep breath, and waited for Omar's response.

"I am so proud of you, Miranda. You have taken everything we talked about and implemented it. Do you have any questions for me? We will continue to meet weekly and continue working on your new skills, but you have the foundation now."

Miranda answered, "Yes, Omar. I do have a question: I came to you because I was feeling insecure and undeserving of my new job. I remember being so afraid of getting caught for being incapable and being fired. You told me I had impostor syndrome, and I eventually agreed. But now we're talking about positive psychology. Does that mean I still have impostor syndrome?"

"Well, do you feel like you do?"

"I guess, in some ways, yes, but not like I did on the first day we met. That was a really tough time for me."

"Okay, well, in our next session, let's talk about how these two important concepts merge together, and ultimately how positive psychology has helped you, and will continue to help you and others, defeat impostor syndrome."

"Alright, I can't wait. See you soon."

~~~

In their next session, Omar jumped right in. "I'm going to ask you to answer a few questions today about impostor syndrome, positive psychology, and how you think one might impact the other."

"Okay, I'm ready."

"Let's start with positive emotions. How do you think practicing positive emotions helps decrease impostor syndrome?"

"Well, it definitely helps to change my thought process. You called that reframing. So, when something goes wrong, I'm learning to change the way I view it. This helped me a lot."

"Mm, hmm…"

"Also, practicing gratitude. This is huge. I'm learning to be grateful for the skills I do have and the opportunities presented to me, rather than dwelling on my shortcomings or what I want to do differently. That has helped me a lot, and focusing on it has helped me understand that I'm more capable of things than I realize."

"What about engagement?"

"I'm learning to focus my work on things that are exciting to me. I try to get 'in the flow' as often as I can and have conversations with Tom about work that entices me. And I do the same thing with my team, I have conversations as frequently as I can and talk about their strengths and what excites them. I think focusing on each of our strengths takes attention away from the things that we're not so good at. That causes me to feel very capable, and therefore I experience less impostor syndrome."

"I love that. What about relationships?"

"Oh man… connection. In one word, connection. I feel like I am supported by the relationships I'm building. I have you, I have Tom, I have my entire team. I also have the impostor syndrome working group, and that alone gives me comfort in knowing I am not alone.

"You know, Omar, I think that building relationships has helped me to think more about other people and not just myself, and by doing that, I'm realizing that the world is so much bigger than just me."

"Human connection. Such a simple and powerful tool." Omar smiled. "And meaning?"

"I ask myself at the end of each workday: What did I do today that mattered? Having an answer to this has helped me realize that even some of the most menial tasks are important. I used to think that my work wasn't *all* that important, but now I realize how much of a role I play at work, at home, and in my community. It makes me feel important and valuable."

"Wonderful. And the last one, accomplishments."

"I think that someone who is struggling with impostor syndrome has a really hard time celebrating themselves. They just don't think they are deserving, or at least that's how I've felt. I've started finding something to celebrate every day, even if it's something as small as bringing my empty coffee cup to the kitchen when I'm finished at the end of the workday. I just feel so much better about starting the next morning with a clean desk. I know that sounds silly…"

"Not at all, Miranda. How does this help with impostor syndrome?"

"I feel deserving, even if I do it for myself. I am deserving of a clean desk, and when I see it each morning, it reminds me of that. I start my day thinking I am deserving and am able to build on that concept. I finally understand it; celebrating myself and my accomplishments gives me self-worth."

"You got it. You can see how just some of the concepts you've learned are tied directly to defeating impostor syndrome. Now that you've said that all out loud, how do you feel?"

"I feel better than I ever have in my career. I know that impostor syndrome is still a part of who I am, and I need to continue practicing positive psychology, but I am more confident than ever that I will eventually defeat it.

I will also add that I feel generally calmer, I'm worrying less, and I feel more confident in myself. At times, I feel like I could take on the world. They are fleeting moments, but I've never had those feelings before, so I hope that if I continue practicing positive psychology, I can continue to improve those positive feelings. No pun intended." Miranda winked and continued on.

"I also remember you telling me that improving both of these scores can also improve job satisfaction, career satisfaction, exhaustion, health, and life satisfaction. I already feel like I'm feeling better in all of these areas, too. I suppose now my goal is also to continue improving my overall well-being, which encompasses all of these areas."

"And you will, Miranda. The key here is consistency. Repetition is important to build a habit. If you practice positive psychology every day, it will eventually become so natural that you won't even know you are doing it. But it's also important to remember that impostor syndrome never goes away. You are going to have to manage this your entire life, and I know you will."

"Oh gosh, yes, I will. I don't want to pretend anymore. I don't want to fake it, and doubt myself, and think I'm undeserving. I want to be authentic. I want to be me."

"You've always been you, Miranda. You were just covered up with a veil of impostor syndrome. And now you have the skills to defeat that."

"I have one more question, Omar: do you think I could apply this to other areas of my life? Sometimes, I feel like I'm an impostor as a parent and a wife. I recently started Pilates, and I have no idea what I'm doing. I'm in the beginners class, but I feel the same way as I did when I started this new role."

"Well, what do you think, Miranda?"

"Okay, okay. I get it. I can, and I will apply positive psychology to all areas of my life."

"You got it. Now go get out there and show impostor syndrome who's really in charge of your life."

~~~

Two years after Miranda's big promotion, an even bigger role opened up: a Vice President role. Miranda knew who had been in the role previously, and they had done a phenomenal job. She also knew that she could handle the job and do it well. She spent a few days working on her resume, highlighting accomplishments and results that she would have previously thought were just a matter of luck.

There was still some skepticism and doubt in her mind as she uploaded her polished resume and hit the 'Apply' button, but she was able to use her new skills and push her feelings to the side. She had never felt more like herself or trusted herself more than she did now. She was invited for several interviews, where she went prepared, confident, and full of authenticity. Her time with Omar learning about positive psychology became one of the things she was most grateful for.

A month later, she accepted the new job.

Key Lessons

I hope you have found Miranda's story to be encouraging. She, like so many people, spent much of her life struggling with impostor syndrome, but by using the five pillars of positive psychology, she was able to defeat her feelings and thrive. Positive psychology is meant to support one's overall well-being and focus on the things that are going well in one's life, instead of the negative. Using her new skills, Miranda was able to also positively impact her life satisfaction, career satisfaction, job satisfaction, exhaustion, and health, which had historically been negatively impacted by impostor syndrome. Here are the key takeaways from her story.

Impostor Syndrome

Impostor syndrome feels like being a fake, hiding one's own success, being afraid of getting caught for pretending to be more capable than one believes they are, and undeserving of success. Someone with impostor syndrome can be defined as having an unhealthy response to success.

People around the world struggle with impostor syndrome every day and it can impact anyone. It doesn't discriminate against gender, race, ethnicity, religion, or even one's position in a company. While impostor syndrome isn't commonly known to ever 'go away,' it can be managed with the proper tools over one's lifetime.

Positive Emotions

Practicing positive emotions is the focus of energy on one's positive emotions, not negative emotions, from an event, situation, or circumstance. This can be done by reframing our thoughts to turn negative thoughts into positive. In addition, a strong focus on frequent gratitude and what went well in one's day, week, month, and so on can help to improve positive emotions.

Positive Engagement

When someone is 'in the flow,' they are experiencing positive engagement. To be 'in the flow,' a person needs to feel like they have lost track of time and are unaware of their surroundings, completely engaged in what they are doing. To accomplish being 'in the flow' means that one is working on tasks, projects, and work that is intrinsically motivating to them and uses their strengths to their maximum potential. It is important to have discussions with each other about work that is most engaging for each person to be sure they are able to get 'in the flow.'

Positive Relationships

Positive relationships in the workplace are those relationships that consistently bring each other up, listen to each other, support each other, and help each other to further their careers and life. Having a best friend at work is a common question to determine how strong one's relationships at work might be, although it is not the only indicator. To practice positive relationships, it is important to pay attention to how one communicates, both verbally and non-verbally. Practicing team building, bonding, inclusivity, and creativity all help to build connection, as does practicing acts of kindness.

Positive Meaning

To feel positive meaning implies that one feels a larger connection and purpose to their team, organization, community, and the world. In the workplace, it is important to remember how one's work contributes beyond just day-to-day tasks. This can be accomplished by the organization or individual getting involved in the community, and reminding each other of how their organization contributes to the well-being of their community, and ultimately the world. Asking *What did I do today that mattered?* is a great tool for practicing positive meaning.

Positive Accomplishments

To practice positive accomplishments, one needs to not only celebrate, they need to set SMART goals for themselves. With SMART goals, it is important to celebrate milestones along the way, and give appropriate feedback to each other when an accomplishment is met. It is important to celebrate both individual successes and team successes, and frequent, even daily, celebrations are encouraged to practice positive accomplishments.

Reflecting on Key Lessons

Understanding Impostor Syndrome

In your journal, freeform your thoughts, good and/or bad, on different tactics you have used to manage impostor syndrome. Here are a few prompts to get you started:

1. In your own words, describe what impostor syndrome feels like for you and how it has impacted your career.

2. Which tactics, methods, or forms of treatment have you used in the past to help manage your impostor syndrome?

3. Which of these worked best for you?

4. What did you learn about yourself and impostor syndrome from undergoing this tactic or method to help defeat impostor syndrome?

5. Describe what it will feel like for you when you defeat impostor syndrome.

Practicing Positive Psychology

In your journal, list as many practices as you can that you, your team, or your organization are already doing related to positive psychology in your daily life. To enhance this activity, do it separately for each of the five pillars of positive psychology – positive emotions, engagement, relationships, meaning, and accomplishments. These do not have to be specific practices listed in this book, but rather methods, tactics, and tools that are helping you to practice psychology in your daily work. Be specific and expand on scenarios where each practice helped you.

Now, list three more *new* methods, tactics, or tools that you are going to implement in your life. Again, these do not have to be specific to this book, but rather new ideas or concepts that you believe will help you to better practice positive emotions in your daily work. If possible, think of and write down a specific scenario where you might be able to practice your idea or concept.

Acknowledgements

Thank you to every professor, researcher, and participant who has been a part of my work and helped me to create something that will help people who struggle with impostor syndrome.

Thank you to every leader and every team member I have had the great fortune of working with over the course of my career. You have all taught me about my own struggles with impostor syndrome and that letting go of them can allow us all to thrive.

Thank you to my editors, Turnedpagesco, who helped me to turn my research into a beautifully written business fable. Your creative work and patience are admirable.

Thank you to each and every beta reader. Your constructive feedback has made my book a masterpiece.

Finally, thank you to Tony, my life partner, and my family for your never-ending support.

About the Author

 Dr. Renee Bruns is a former Fortune 500 executive who has struggled with impostor syndrome her entire life. She is also a mental health advocate and believes strongly in the power of positive psychology. She received an undergraduate degree in psychology, a master's degree in business administration, and a doctorate in business administration, where she combined her passions with her workplace struggles for her research project. Her dissertation topic was "The Impacts of Coaching and Positive Psychology on Impostor Syndrome in the Workplace."

Dr. Bruns believes that all people can defeat impostor syndrome and live enriching lives that feel authentic to them, and that everyone deserves a life where impostor syndrome doesn't dominate. This book is her way of showing others how to be positive with themselves, others, and the world around them, to kick impostor syndrome to the side.

References

[i] Clance, P. R., & Imes, S. A. (1978). The imposter phenomenon in high achieving women: Dynamics and therapeutic intervention. *Psychotherapy: Theory, Research & Practice, 15*(3), 241–247. https://doi.org/10.1037/h0086006

[ii] Young, V. (2022). *The 5 Types of Impostor Syndrome. Impostor Syndrome Institute.* https://impostorsyndrome.com/articles/5-types-of-impostor-syndrome/

[iii] Hutchins, H. M., Penney, L. M., & Sublett, L. W. (2018). What imposters risk at work: Exploring imposter phenomenon, stress coping, and job outcomes. *Human Resource Development Quarterly, 29*(1), 31–48. https://doi.org/10.1002/hrdq.21304

[iv] McDowell, W. C. (2015). *The Impact of Self-Efficacy and Perceived Organizational Support on the Imposter Phenomenon.*

[v] Bernard, N. S., Dollinger, S. J., & Ramaniah, N. V. (2002). Applying the Big Five Personality Factors to the Impostor Phenomenon. Journal of Personality Assessment, 78(2), 321–333. https://doi.org/10.1207/S15327752JPA7802_07

[vi] Booth, S. (n.d.). *What Is Imposter Syndrome?* WebMD. Retrieved December 15, 2024, from https://www.webmd.com/balance/what-is-imposter-syndrome

[vii] Bravata, D. M., Watts, S. A., Keefer, A. L., Madhusudhan, D. K., Taylor, K. T., Clark, D. M., Nelson, R. S., Cokley, K. O., & Hagg, H. K. (2020). Prevalence, Predictors, and Treatment of Impostor Syndrome: A Systematic Review. *Journal of General Internal Medicine, 35*(4), 1252–1275. https://doi.org/10.1007/s11606-019-05364-1

[viii] Magro, C. (2022). From hiding to sharing. A descriptive phenomenological study on the experience of being coached for impostor syndrome. *International Journal of Evidence Based Coaching & Mentoring*, 68–80. https://doi.org/10.24384/0409-b325

[ix] Seligman, M. E. P. (2011). *Flourish: A visionary new understanding of happiness and well-being* (1st Free Press hardcover ed). Free Press.

[x] Seligman, M. E. P., & Csikszentmihalyi, M. (2000). *Positive psychology: An introduction. American Psychologist, 55*(1), 5–14. https://doi.org/10.1037/0003-066X.55.1.5

[xi] Positive Psychology Timeline. (2013, October 11). *Live Happy.* https://livehappy.com/resources/positive-psychology-timeline/